Levity

Levity

Finding Magic in a World of Logic

Guru Singh

Guru Singh -- born in 1945 -- is a third-generation yoga master -- a master teacher of Kundalini Yoga, Meditation, Mantra and 'Humanology'. He is also a musician, composer, author, artist, husband and father, and Minister of Sikh Dharma. He is based in Los Angeles and Seattle. He met Yogi Bhajan (master of Kundalini and Tantric yoga) in January of 1969 and has been teaching, from this ancient lineage, throughout the world since 1970. He studied Western music beginning at the age of five and Eastern music caught his ear when he was nineteen. Guru Singh's classes are filled with deeply creative and inspiring music and mantra. He has published several books and mantra albums over the years. You can find this music, the books and his lectures online at www.gurusingh.com and the daily prayers @gurusinghyogi on Instagram.

Editors:
Guruperkarma Kaur Khalsa
Tamara Grace Arjanpreet Kaur

Cover Design:
Kendall Guilburt (photograph & design)
Arvind Singh (layout & design)

Back Cover Design:
Arvind Singh (layout & design)
Marc Royce (photograph)

Creative and Production Design
Arvind Singh

Produced by ReEvolution Books — A division of Guru Singh Inc.
© Guru Singh Inc. 2016
ISBN-13: 9781530355495
ISBN-10: 1530355494

Dedication

There's a natural desire to dedicate one's achievements to the countless people who help make them possible . . . for the moments that make up the momentum . . . enabling everything within the achievement to take place. Here, to name a few, I dedicate this work to those who've walked with me through the years of these pages, stories and parables . . . as they built our awareness of how the 'magic' of life mixes with the 'logic' . . . allowing 'levity' to exist and persist.

I dedicate this project to my parents and sister, Bert, Tidi and Vickie, the first yogis to influence my world . . . and to their teachers. I also dedicate this to the greatest teacher in my life, Yogi Bhajan, and to his wife who was always there by his side. Together they taught my wife and me to stand by each other through everything. These daily prayers actually started some years ago when Yogi Bhajan's wife, Bhai Sahiba Dr. Bibiji Inderjit Kaur, needed prayers . . . she ignited the daily inspirations that now make up the pages of this book. I also dedicate this to their children, who taught us all -- from day one -- how to handle the constant unknowns that come with any vast system of teachings: their eldest son, Sardar Ranbir Singh Bhai; their middle son, Bhai Sahib Kulbir Singh

Puri, and their daughter, Sardarni Kamaljit Kaur . . . each one has shared so much -- especially the family qualities of their father's mastery.

I dedicate this to my wife, Guruperkarma Kaur; our son, Sopurkh Singh; our daughter, her husband, and their daughter (plus another one ready to be born) Haripurkh Kaur, Scott MacGowan and Narayan Kaur, plus . . . .

Of course there are so many others . . . there always are. May GOD bless every one of you who stands within the teachings of all great wisdom . . . this will, most certainly over time, activate the loving hearts, and the higher minds of humanity.

Foreword

These prayers are a fabric, woven from 'word-threads', holding spacetime channels open in the traditions of true nature. It's an illuminating response to the way human nature has been wandering and meandering off course for well over a hundred thousand years. The glorious nature of these 'word-threads' is that it can open the mouth of time; fill your heart with vastness; ignite your brain's inspiration with deep inquisition . . . the curiosity that gives you the authority to sing your own words out over the ocean; from the tops of the mountains . . . and then soar. As a matter of course, when you read these pages, the 'word-threads' can make possibilities out of your impossibilities, they can inspire you to unfold the potential of your highest heights. The lotus does this in the mud . . . growing spotlessly above the dirt that nourishes it. Practicing the use of your own 'word-threads' allows you to be exactly who you are . . . as you are . . . which is enough . . . it's always enough. They allow your everlasting flow to listen to your ever-present Soul . . . it speaks in never ending prose . . . so poetically. These following pages present reverent simplicities of the ancient wisdom-keepers speaking from spirit . . . sacredness arriving in your heart with each phrase. They give you options; alternative views of this and every moment of time . . . they lift you up out of the mud with their levity.

Kendall A Guilburt -- March 16, 2016
Artist for 'Levity' -- the book

The Chapters

In the late 1960's and early 1970's the world of Kundalini Yoga -- outside of India -- was just getting started . . . Ashrams and Yoga Centers popping up all over the world. Yogi Bhajan (Master of Kundalini Yoga) was sending out teachers . . . I was always there, right by his side, wishing and hoping to be sent somewhere too. He would constantly turn to me and say, "You're staying right here . . . you must learn to go nowhere." And so it was, year in and year out, I stayed right where I was, but I was also his everything guy . . . fixed the roof; washed the car; drove the car; tended the garden; reshaped the windows; built the sheds . . . all right there. Back in those days it rained in Los Angeles, and it would always rain at night. Every night when the storms would come in, the roof on Yogi Bhajan's home, at the center known as Guru Ram Das Ashram, would spring a leak. Midnight, 1am, 2am . . . my phone would ring . . . "Guru Singh . . . roof is leaking again!" The routine would begin . . . on with my cloths . . . into my car, and three miles later I'd arrive at "the leaky roof" . . . wiggle on my back into the crawl space . . . find the "hole" and patch it . . . over and over again. One morning, the call came through . . . the routine began . . . but forty five minutes later, the call came again . . . I answered with extreme anger . . . "Yeah, what?" Frozen silence filled the phone line . . . then a soft voice finally came through . . . "Guru Singh, is that you?" "Yes," I answered, still angry, "I can't find my keys." There was another long moment of silence on the phone -- then Yogi Bhajan very quietly and calmly said, "Ask your hands . . . they are the last ones to have touched them . . . they know, but be very quiet, because they speak softly." I did . . . I got quiet . . . within a few minutes a picture arrived in my senses -- exactly where the last contact had been made. Our prayer is that you listen consciously and locate all the moments and mementos that are precious to you; remain connected with everyone and everything you love; relate to the subtleties that know where everything is, and enjoy all the wise discoveries.

Whenever you've missed an opportunity, remember that time is a wave, and a wave behaves like this -- the wave itself travels through the water, but the water remains in place. Therefore, when the next wave arrives, the opportunity is there again . . . if you're open to it. When you're fully aware as each moment arrives, you'll recognize when it returns. This is one of the many benefits of increased awareness, being able to spot the return of an opportunity, rather than being upset by having missed it the first time around. In this understanding of physics, you're able to enjoy the "reality" behind the "illusion" of time. In every moment you have thousands of micro-thoughts and micro-choices -- these are behind the obvious display of the ones you know. These accumulate to build attitudes and moods . . . the attitude of either being disappointed, or hopeful when an opportunity is missed. When you've done what it takes to become 'super-aware' -- every missed opportunity is a signal to watch for the return. When you do not operate with this level of awareness, your disappointment puts you into an attitude and mood that controls your subsequent moments. Then, in your frustration, you deny the possibility of having what you've missed. This accumulates -- controls your micro-thoughts and micro-choices -- builds attitudes and moods of expecting to miss out . . . now you're all setup to fulfill this negative prophecy . . . and you will. The psycho-emotional body would rather be "right" than fulfilled . . . a nature derived from its days of survival . . . when every "right" was a live or die moment. To change this visible reality -- discipline your micro-reality -- all the thoughts and choices occurring in the background. Discipline yourself to not be controlled by mood -- ride the ever returning wave of time toward fulfillment. Our prayer is that you understand the physics of existence; live in this higher awareness, not your lower, survival, protective moods; build a momentum from all of your missed opportunities and fulfill your dreams . . . expect the best . . . it's always there . . . or soon will be.

*F*or a hundred thousand years, due to evolutionary pressures, the relationship between humans and time has become a progression of ever increasing chaos. Today, people are consumed with efforts to rewrite the past and control the future . . . with never enough time. The present moment has been completely vacated at the present moment. Physicists have studied the "flow" of time in this Universe, and they now propose what the great masters have taught for thousands of years. The "Big Bang" produced multiple universes, some of which are inverse mirrors to this one. In these, time unfolds in the opposite direction: it moves backwards . . . older becomes younger, ends become beginnings. When surrounded by the perspective of that "version" of time -- because time is a total emersion -- it would appear that the time here on Earth was moving backwards, not forwards. This is only one way that time is an illusion. It's not a constant . . . it's completely mutable. Science also believes that time is not something that pre-exists, but it begins at a central point and flows out in all directions. Then the masters ask, "Where is the central point? What has existed before this beginning?" If instead of this, as a conscious master, you sit in absolute stillness . . . and in the perfection of this absoluteness no time passes at all. All time becomes a single moment and its passage is the illusion of your observation in motion, but you're still. Then, when it does appear to be moving, you're aware of the moment entering the moment. It passes through the Atlas and Axis vertebra in your neck on its way to the lungs and heart with the rib cage holding each moment as a breath. In this awareness of time, your body knows every goal will be achieved. This knowing then understands the amount of time it will take. Our prayer is that you find this peace and calm in your "version" of time; completely realign your desires to become the certainties of absolute knowing, in the ease of this relation, use joy as motivation, and "pass" some of your time in stillness without passage.

When you welcome a newborn into this world, and the child's consciousness detaches from the 'etheric realm' to fully focus on the physical body in the process of birthing, there's great celebration all around the new member of the family. At this very same moment, there's also been a death in the etheric realm, and great mourning is taking place on that level of Spirit while the three dimensional celebration fills the Earthly space with joy. Likewise, when a person passes from this world, when they transfer back through to those etheric dimensions -- in the midst of the grieving here on Earth, there's great celebration amongst the angels . . . welcoming the return of a member of the 'eternal family' from their "time" within "time" here on Earth. This 'eternal family' is your tribe; it's filed with so many of your friends, your relatives, children, lovers, some enemies, and of course the angels who cycle back and forth even more rapidly as your pets. Death is something that's completely misunderstood by most modern cultures, and completely understood by the traditional indigenous ones. There's a poem that goes: "Everything's dying to be reborn; infant day is the early morn; brightly moving through the day to end; into the night where it's born again." Everything is dying to be reborn into another form . . . it's the wisdom of knowing these various forms that allows for celebration to accompany the mourning. The process of mourning is an honest and authentic process -- it's the very real severing and releasing of physical connections and attachments so that Spirit connections can replace them . . . without this grieving in four dimensions, the other dimensions remain unnoticed. Our prayer is that when it's time to grieve, you enthusiastically grieve without reservation; release the familiarity and welcome the unknown; be ready for a rush of joy that arrives with Spirit, for this is the omniscient and omnipresent nature of all rebirthing . . . it's the realm of angels.

When you gaze at the nighttime sky it can seem impressive and massive -- but all you're actually viewing is a small part of the local neighborhood . . . the part you see with the naked eye is tiny by comparison to what's really out there. On the very best of nights, you see about 2,500 stars . . . roughly one hundred-millionth of the stars just in the Milky Way galaxy alone. And almost all of them are less than 1,000 light years away . . . only 1% of the Milky Way's diameter. Much of what appears as a star in the sky, is a galaxy of billions of stars, appearing as a single object within your eyes. As many stars as there are in this galaxy -- 100 to 400 billion -- there are roughly an equal number of galaxies in the observable universe, using the most powerful telescopes. For every star in this Milky Way galaxy, there's another entire galaxy out there. Think about it in another way, for every grain of sand on Earth, there are 10,000 stars in the sky. The percentage of those stars that are "sun-like" (similar in size, temperature, and luminosity to your sun) using the most conservative thinking -- is around 5%. This means that there are -- in the most limited of estimates -- 500 quintillion, or 500 (billion billion) "sun-like" stars out there with systems potentially containing a twin to this Earth . . . one hundred Earth-like planets for every grain of sand in the world. Our prayer is that -- with all that's going on in your world -- you take a moment to think about what might be going on beyond your world; that you understand your issues are not as intimidating as you think, and by shifting your thoughts you can shift your life. Allow yourself to become inclusive in your thinking so that the vastness of where you actually live, alters the way you actually live; that being the change you want to see, means changing the way you see the changes . . . they're not so daunting after all . . . just a grain of sand on the beach of your mind.

All life is a network -- a cooperative -- and according to the UN World Food Organization, Earth's current agricultural potential can feed at least twelve billion people. Even with all the challenges we have with water and land, the Earth is still abundant; it's prepared to feed every child, every woman, and every man alive. But this would require that food not be considered a commodity, but a rightful necessity; that food pricing not be subject to commodity speculation, and all food be distributed as an obligation directly connected to the privilege of being alive. Currently this is not the case . . . global food is a market where prices are set by commodity speculators . . . distribution is determined by the highest bidders, and profit literally controls who lives and who dies of starvation. Every single day on Earth, twenty-seven thousand people starve to death . . . mostly children. The human species does not adhere to any natural balance when it comes to the distribution of food . . . all other creatures are oriented toward group prosperity . . . the largest numbers thrive with tremendous fairness and equality . . . this is the way of nature. But not the current human nature -- far from being the most advanced creature on this planet -- humans, are in many ways, the babies, the emotionally underdeveloped creatures in the evolutionary cycle. "Free-will" -- the ability of the human to step outside the commanding balance of nature -- creates its own nature. The ability to compassionately apply "free-will" is the challenge that faces humanity as life evolves. By caring for this planet in holistic terms; by experiencing what happens to others as a measure of the total health; by compassionately working for prosperity in every life -- not the profits of lifeless capital . . . no one would be suffering the indignation of starvation. Our prayer is that you take your place in the abundant life; open your "free-will" to create solutions for all life to prosper; evolve as an example -- become an adult -- be a parent to humanity -- create a compelling influence for others to follow -- make absolutely certain everyone is eating . . . this is a place to start . . . this is the basis of life . . . you alone can make a difference together.

*I*n ancient yogic teachings, moments were measured in what they called taals . . . the rhythms and coordination of the breaths and heartbeats -- either 3/4 or 4/4 based timings. 3/4 is the rhythm of the heart, and 4/4 is the rhythm of the brain. Your ability to absorb and make sense of life is determined by these rhythms . . . your experience is always based on the attitude of your inhale, and the voice you attach to each exhale. 3/4 is the timing of a waltz . . . the music of the heart . . . it draws people together. 4/4 is the timing of a march, and other classical compositions . . . these rhythms draw your thoughts together . . . they clarify the mind. In the late 1970's, it was discovered that classical music, in 4/4 time, was the best to play in the background when you're studying and absorbing information . . . it's called 'super-learning' and music systems were developed. Think of your life -- you always have a variety of tasks before you . . . tasks that require connections, and other tasks that require individual clarity. There are also moments that require both individual clarity and togetherness. Something to watch for when there's this combined need for clarity within togetherness . . . mental clarity can be critical in nature; critical natures are disruptive to togetherness. 'Clarity with togetherness' requires a unique balance between your heart and your head . . . you must literally be breathing in something divisible by both a 3 and 4 . . . the ancient musicians developed a powerful rhythm of 12 for this purpose. This is also the very tuning of nature . . . a year is divided by 12, with 4 seasons of 3 months each; the zodiac is divided into 12 signs, with 4 elements of 3 signs each; a day has 12 hours, as does the night . . . all of these are measures of moments that need both clarity and togetherness. Our prayer is that you create conscious rhythms in every moment of your life; with your breathing, connect your moment to live in clarity; approach every day to achieve what it's there for, and live your life as a mastery, not a mystery . . . find comfort in the yogic discipline of consciously breathing.

*H*umansarepsycho-emotionallyinfluencedbyculturalopinions -- the memes that pass themselves off as authorities of some "authority." These are the psychic persuasions that have been lurking in the background of the human conversation, some for decades; others for centuries; some even for millennia. Since you -- as a conscious being -- are attempting to release these barbaric, unnatural natures; to become real, to be calm, centered and aware -- it's essential to first realize and acknowledge these psychic persuasions as part of the collective, historical, human experience. But then, do what you can to release them from your own patterns. It's like when 'fire-making' was first discovered to be possible -- the fire-makers were a huge disruption to the tradition of all the fire-keepers . . . even perhaps, at times, the claim was of fraud -- that 'man-made' fire was not real fire -- or -- that no one has the right to make fire. There's a similar obsession in the current psycho-emotional meme . . . a series of highly modeled cultural opinions being "crowd" reinforced over and over to create "truths" that aren't true. You have to be very aware to catch this "sleight of hand" and by design most people are not aware. These are the cards dealt to this moment of history; your task is to live in this darkness -- this most superficial and corrupted of times, and be the fire-maker . . . warm, inviting and revelatory. In order to start your own fires, and shine light into this darkness, you must release the darkness of your own hesitations . . . you must release the idea that you don't have the right . . . then ride the winds of this new authority into your mastery. You'll feel strange in a strange land at first, but keep up, and you'll be kept up. Our prayer is that your courage comes to your aid right now; that you constantly start your own fires, and know that you have every right to do so . . . and do so with a humungous joy that includes every one . . . even the big doubters.

*H*uman evolution developed an appropriate instinct to be civil. Over long periods of time, however, this led to an assortment of "being nice" mechanisms. The drawback to these "being nice" mechanisms is that they also developed dishonesty. Being "nice" without being honest became a part of human style. The real art form in life would be to be "nice" and honest simultaneously but the efficiencies in the evolution of instincts tied these ancient relation protocols together into manners. These manners have been active in human cultures for thousands of years and they now appear as mandates. They've been used to determining hierarchies and maintaining social positioning, and eventually they've maintained false 'pecking-orders' in the order of importance. The true nature of life is that all life is equal and it is all of equal importance. So naturally when hierarchies are enabled, the manners and protocols that follow are social dishonesty and the differences are false to begin with. This false process dates back to times (in the hunt) when you were competing for positions in the "order" of things to determine survival. Today this dishonesty is unhealthy, not only on the macro (inter-personal) level, but also to your body cells. Every cell, of any physical system, knows when there's even slight dishonesty anywhere in the system. The moment this is detected, cells go into tension and replace ease with dis-ease. This is exactly how a lie-detector machine works . . . it senses tension. Masking this dishonesty -- beyond the point of self-recognition -- has become a learned skill. Protocols, social positioning and hierarchies are based upon it and it has become a human goal. Our prayer is that you realize you were born to break these patterns; honesty comes first, and whatever protocols you maintain in addition to this are way down the list of importance. This is why the masters said that apology and forgiveness are the super-skills of life. They're essential when you're being "brutally" honest. Our prayer is that you master these skills; that you are always "brutally" honest, and masterfully compassionate at the same time.

*E*very celestial object, even the Earth, produces a distinct sound . . . a frequency . . . a tone . . . the sound of its existence. The Earth's tone is called the Schumann resonance, after Dr. Schumann who discovered its 7.83Hz frequency in the early 1950's. What produces these sounds in very large celestial objects . . . the sounds of space? They're made up of vibrational waves from the various forces in the realm of empty space; the multitude of heavenly bodies interacting; the electromagnetic pulses given off by these objects, their rings, and their moons; the radio waves that bounce between them and their invisible borders of stratospheres and atmospheres; the interaction of charged particles within their atmospheres, and the energetics that encircle the objects; the rotational spin, orbit, and even the stellar and galactic winds. This is a huge formula that goes into these celestial sounds. Your being requires this resonance, this sound, in order to understand its physical, emotional and mental place in spacetime. It operates like a guide and a guard to your entire system. This need was first discovered when the early astronauts were returning from orbit, after prolonged periods outside this influence, and were completely disoriented. It was the Russian Cosmonaut program that invented a Schumann resonator to compensate for this absence in space. The actions that produce the greatest connection for tuning you into this resonance are -- grounding . . . being in actual contact with the

Earth as much as possible . . . walking barefoot on the ground. Our prayer is that you tune into the body of Mother Earth every day; that you ground yourself and maintain this connection with daily discipline; that you're in touch with the Mother like your healthy life depends on it . . . because it does.

The chemistry of sacred -- the driving force of all life -- is found in the longing to belong, to connect to that which surrounds you. This is the 'relate and exchange' routine of all authentic communication . . . this will always be somewhat disruptive because it's so vital and deeply honest. The noise of indoctrination is what programs us to lose touch with this honest chemistry of the sacred. Cerebral spinal taps have revealed that there's a distinct photonic-crystal structure in the fluid that flows in the spine and surrounds the brain . . . this is the source that actually communicates this honest longing within and around the physical body. The band of frequencies found in this fluid's communication are identical to the ones found directed between the most powerful stellar light energies. In other words, the same frequencies that cause you to want to connect with one another, are the frequencies that connect the stars together in this Universe. These nano-crystal fluids are also responsible for carrying the optical portion of the kundalini rising . . . which is the largest portion of all the kundalini activity. Here you have it -- your Kundalini rising is the same frequency as the stars connecting -- is the same frequency as your desire to be a part of the whole -- is the key to your higher consciousness, and the chemistry of the sacred . . . all is one. Our prayer is that you constantly rejuvenate this crystalline fluid through yoga, prayer, meditation, music, dance, breath and joy; that you believe in your authority to create your own stardom, and that you're at peace within the noise that naturally surrounds this chemistry of sacredness . . . it's just the reaction that's equal to your sacred actions.

The heart teaches you to exert when you're giving and then relax in order to receive. Most people operate in the exact reverse way to this . . . exerting to get is the most common reason for working. However, when you exert to get, you never actually experience the sensation of receiving -- not actual receiving . . . this then binds you to the constant effort of working to get, and sensing the emptiness of not receiving . . . such is the core to the malady called greed . . . "the constant struggle to receive." The masterful heart, that teaches how to abundantly receive without being greedy, is surrounded by two other great teachers . . . these are the lungs. The lungs are always quite filled -- this is their natural state when at rest -- you have to work hard to completely empty them. Whenever you fully relax, they fill back up . . . they are naturally fulfilled. Masters have known for millennia -- and science is quickly learning -- within each breath of these lungs, are the answers to each moment; the solutions to the problems are within this state of fulfillment. The breath doesn't hold the infinite information, it holds the infinite reference, and the inference is your quest . . . this is all the filter. The combination of this filter and your breathing produces the information of the answers and the solutions . . . when you relax, you receive this . . . this is the basic nature of faith and confidence. Our prayer is that you use these natural heartfelt realities to achieve that which you want to receive; live in faith . . . the greed-free prosperity of your every breath . . . confident, that you are so fortunate . . . that the infinite, will take care of it . . . all of it.

We're entering a new era of evolution -- an era that's never been known before . . . we're entering the era of enlightenment. This is not "Pollyanna" -- this is evolution's necessity . . . there's no other way for seven, eight, nine and ten billion people to occupy this small planet without destroying each other in the process, and evolution is reacting. Imagine -- not competing religions -- but twenty million Buddhas; twenty million women and men with the consciousness of Jesus . . . all walking the planet at the same time. Not gathering disciples, for that's the style of the past, but teaching and training anyone who is ready, willing and able, to reach this same level of awakening . . . sharing their enlightenment, not protecting it as the secrets of a power base. This new time is without competition and comparison, it's about compassion and openly sharing the wealth of wisdom. This is evolution reacting to the times we're currently experiencing . . . times of distrust, of competition and violence. This is not about idealism, it's about the balance that always prevails in the material universe . . . it's the reaction, reacting to the current actions. Not a moment too soon either . . . the Earth is collapsing under this violent pressure -- seven-plus billion people all competing for space and resources is clearly not working. This new time will not take place without disruption -- this disruption and violence are the driving "triggers" that keep the solution evolving. And as this solution evolves, everything that's found power in secrecy and exclusivity will feel threatened . . . when the powerful feel threatened they use their power to protect their exclusivity. This is the root of the violence we're currently experiencing. But as this new renaissance unfolds, the differences will become the opportunities. Our prayer is that you see this coming, and you see yourself as a leader in this evolving solution; that you see this as the natural reaction to the current activities of violence and never lose hope . . . this new era is fast approaching and you're one of the reasons why . . . you're just in time.

*M*aking mistakes is a sign of growth; of trying something new, or unusual. Making mistakes must be rewarded as much as the rewards for getting things right. There can never be growth without trying something new and therefore there cannot be growth without mistakes. Our prayer is that you make mistakes and grow with loving each one of them.

*O*ver the past few months the Earth has smashed through centuries of global temperature records by margins beyond scientific imagination. This new data released by NASA, has led scientists to call this global trend a "climate emergency". These same trends were in the prehistory of this planet . . . a time of massive instability; extinctions of untold magnitude, and conditions everywhere that were unable to consistently sustain life . . . we've entered this "twilight zone" once again. Science warned the people of Earth to not exceed 350 particles per million (ppm) of CO_2 . . . lost in a meaningless debate of denial, you blew through that barrier without a blink and are now at 400 ppm . . . heading toward 600 ppm by the end of this century. 600 ppm was Earth 32.8 million years ago . . . the oceans globally are 60 meters higher . . . that's 200 feet. The continental coastlines will be under water by the end of this century and it's too late to stop it . . . this includes much of New York, Washington DC and many other 'vital' coastal cities. Where will the people and the infrastructure be moved to, and how destructive will the move be? With changes of this magnitude about to shock the world, it's time for you to shock your own world, refuse to spend a single moment wrestling with, or worrying about the "deniers" -- they're simply "innocent-ignorant" children without a clue of awareness. Spend your valuable time increasing your intuitive skills -- you're going to need them far sooner than imagined, for with a "climate emergency" comes all sorts of other emergencies. You'll be called upon to make time sensitive decisions within a completely uncertain future time . . . be prepared . . . you're a pioneer in a completely new reality. Humanity will soon run out of its "way of life" -- one that's been evolving and improving for eons . . . someone needs to be mindful as these improvements all disappear . . . why not you . . . why not now. Our prayer is that you take this opportunity to become that enlightened pioneer -- not an alarmist, but a realist; show up for this new reality before it's here and be one who can walk and talk this new evolution . . . be a new "first responder."

he outcome of any moment is the combination of your preconception and the insistence within the conception of the moment referred to by the masters as the "what is." There's an additional influence available through your higher consciousness, a "super-condition" at the quantum level within the core of all matter and all moments. This has influence far stronger than preconception, and beyond the insistence of "what is." This is the "super-condition" of knowing that "it's already done." A mantra that perfectly depicts this knowing is: "Humee hum brahm hum" meaning "What is to be, already is." When this third condition is introduced to the other two, you have the traction that guides each moment as if being led by some masterful power beyond time and beyond any preconception; beyond any influence of "what is." With this super-knowing, your desired outcome is just a matter of spending time, which is all you have in life anyway. The famous saying: "It's just a matter of time," works its "magic" and ultimately nothing's impossible. This is the 'knowing' of patience; it replaces all the snarky 'waiting' of patience . . . the outcome of what's "already done" pays you dividends by being done through the time that you spend. As you become more and more aware of these quantum mechanics around you then you can make a decision. You're no longer playing to your reflection, like most everyone does, always being influenced by OPO (other people's opinions). You're going to be your own projection. No more "mirror-mirror on the wall" and no more need for confirmation, validation, or authorization. You are free. Suddenly, the world is filled with similarities -- this is the safety delivered with freedom. Before this freedom of similarities, you're dealing with the scary differences and disappointments like the current nature of human nature. Our prayer is that you believe in this freedom; that you use this patience of knowing to manifest the outcomes within all of your moments, and then allow the momentum of each moment to carry you through the miracle of free time . . . to manifest your desires that are already done.

Intuition -- the exact knowing of a moment -- begins functioning when you accept that you don't know what you know -- for it is then that you allow the information that is everywhere, to be where you are. When you don't claim to know what you know, you bring no pretext into the moment -- then, within the very moment -- the 'what' needs to be known, becomes the 'what' you intuitively know . . . obviously presented in a way that's recognizable to your honest vacancy. At this level of intimacy with your senses, the quality of life is measured with heartbeats and breaths . . . thoughts are noiseless, and your intuition is the attitude within your inhale and the voice of your exhale. The massive indoctrination of social noise in today's world is what pre-programs you, it causes you to lose touch with your -- very natural -- intuitive presence . . . that deep knowing presence that's everywhere and always available. Our prayer is that you practice touching your breaths and heartbeats . . . be with your presence, and without thought . . . lean on your intuitive nature and master each moment, and be in silent peace within all the noise.

*E*verything humans have ever created outside themselves, are things mimicking the world that exists inside. The wheel; the radio; the ability to record light and sound . . . you've replaced telepathy with telephony; the wheel mimics red blood cells rolling through the capillaries; the radio is your thoughts arriving from the constant broadcast of the universal mind. Even the new stealth world -- the redirection of sensory perception . . . they're building meta-materials that can disguise an object until it disappears into the background. It can also be used to mimic the appearance of something else -- this is the nature of maya . . . the nature of shamanic shape-shifting . . . like Harry Potter's invisibility cloak. There's absolutely nothing that's impossible as science explores these depths in the quantum world. You're entering the other side of the exact same Universe . . . this is the magical side. Logic won't explain everything anymore; it's identical to the illusion that you perceive, and the reality that you don't ever see. Imagine this being used for benevolent reasons . . . an object disappears into the background . . . misinformation becomes the new reality to solve problems that were previously unsolvable. Where strong interactions need to work in harmony with each other -- like people in the current world -- this is already taking place inside you at the level of bosons and fermions . . . the sub-atomic particles. An example of a fermion is an electron; a boson is a light particle (photon). These particles can exchange with each other in a sort of alchemy -- transforming into one another: fermions into bosons (bosonization), or reverse it (fermionization) . . . all in the realm that turns intractable problems into completely solvable ones. As science works to find the answers in the outside world, this is already available on world that's inside you. Our prayer is that you begin to know that you have these answers; that you solve problems that are unsolvable because you know that you can; that you become the magician performing magic . . . so clearly needed in this world . . . self-realize that you are the possibility in every impossibility.

*E*ight to Ten thousand years ago, humans began cultivating their food . . . it's had remarkable benefits and significant setbacks. Saving seeds was innovative; it enabled far more predictable food sources, but also sacrificed the human's 'botanical' sense -- a sense that early humans used to understand the difference between nutritional, medicinal, and pathological plants . . . food -- medicine -- poison. Cultivating animals for slaughter has had a profoundly negative affect on the human psycho-emotional consciousness. Caring for a living creature, and then murdering it for food, constitutes a deep betrayal. This introduced emotional disturbances into the collective human psychology, and once introduced -- they reproduced -- as thousands of years passed, these levels of betrayal morphed into other, more compound, emotions. This corrupted atmosphere has become normal and now governs human behavior into what is considered acceptable . . . patterns and attitudes that are found in no other species . . . completely unacceptable to most animals in nature. Humans were never biologically prepared to be murderous carnivores, and are now living with near pathological levels of these patterns and sub-patterns woven throughout their collective consciousness. With this increase in betrayal and aggression, came the escalation of cruelty and revenge as common behavior . . . allowing suffering without concern to affect innocent peoples, cultures, religions, and nations. This hyper-development of inhumane emotions is now firmly in place. Our prayer is that forgiveness, compassion, communication and deep listening (sunia) becomes your habit to slowly and clearly replace this collective pattern that has developed over the millennia. As Gandhi once said, "An eye for an eye and the whole world becomes blind." All humans can rethink their diet and agriculture and reduce the foods that adversely affect the planet . . . to allow the peace that's always been there, to become the peace that's always shared . . . now is the best time to begin.

When you have yourself as your own best friend, you've lost your worst critic. Dishonesty amongst friends is generally a weakness of courage rather than an intention to be false. In the face of such a weakness, it's forgiveness and compassion that returns the relationship to its strength without loss. This is how self-forgiveness is vital in maintaining the value of the best friend self. Maintaining this friendship is at the base of all other relations. Some might claim that this is like being "full of yourself" . . . but take note, being 'full of yourself' is not a bad thing, it's just a 'thing' . . . a 'thing' that can be used to care for others, or boast about yourself. When being 'full of yourself' is used to care for others, your "cup" is overflowing . . . your life is of service. Being of service to others is one of the healthiest investments one can make; healthy, not only to your emotional body, but studies have traced this health into the physical body as well. In fact, being of service to others is a great gift you can give yourself . . . it returns the best friend -- of the self -- to the self in massive quantities. This is when the emotional body is in peak form, and at this level of performance you realize all emotions have purpose. Even intolerance for example . . . intolerance is best used to be intolerant of intolerance. This forces a deeper dive into the root causes of the intolerance that you're intolerant of. Suddenly, in the midst of this deep dive, you're led to self-examination . . . the root cause of others is found within yourself. It's this non-logical state that brings intuitive explanations into the moment . . . the moment speaks for itself because you won't tolerate anything less. This is called self-realization . . . the mastery that's delivered by the best friend self. Our prayer is that you welcome your 'self' as your best friend forever; acknowledge this relationship on a daily basis; then turn all other relations into opportunities for service . . . the return on your investment will be healthy, happy and holy.

*H*urricanes, cyclones and typhoons all come out of the tropics where the rainforest foliage produces the majority of our Earth's oxygen. It's in the swirling turbulence of air in these gigantic storms where the centripetal movement forces the oxygen into the atmosphere. How ironic, these massive and disruptive storms maintain the life sustaining value of our atmosphere. Our prayer is that you are aware of the reasons for all the storms that take place in your life and then build your home with the strength, dynamics and integrity to keep it solid throughout all these life-sustaining events.

*E*xpanding your personal model of time expands the boundaries and measures of your consciousness. By expanding these boundaries, it expands the possibilities and probabilities. This opens the space and time required to turn possible and probably into actual. There's an ancient proverb, when translated it says: "The higher you fly, the greater the much." Time is both space in motion through a point of reference, and a point of reference moving through a volume of space . . . they're inseparable. The space you occupy is a wave in this fabric of time; the time you spend is a wave in the fabric of space. In universal terms, these movements and changes are measured in such vast numbers (billions of Earth years) that it appears to be static, but nothing ever began -- because 'something' was always going on before 'that' -- whatever 'that' is, or was. By realizing -- like the skin on your body – that the surface of the Earth is constantly changing, and the space that surrounds Earth, the sky and the Universe is constantly changing only then can you alter the foundations of your consciousness. You begin to realize that time is forever; it's divided into the moments we perceive; it has always existed with its waves in constant motion. You begin to comprehend that space expands according to the needs of time and the needs of time shift according to the collective beliefs of the space. This is the material basis of the phenomenon of tolerance. To accommodate, you tolerate that which forever accommodates you. When you think and emote beyond the limits of limitation, then all individual beings, the social systems, the ecosystems and the entire material Universe becomes a network of inseparable relationships. Our prayer is that you make a decision to ignore any limits that appear to be there; that you tolerate your limitlessness; accommodate the same in others; realize "reality" is a habit of current thinking . . . patterns in the unexpanded models of time. Expand your model to such a degree that it welcomes the changes that will automatically occur in others . . . "become the change you want to see in this world."

When human beings are present and in their hearts, the women of the world will be able to unfold the future (the womb) of the world with great joy, creativity and confidence. Women have been waiting, not to be equal to men, but to be given peaceful moments where it's safe to bring the future moments into this moment. Women are the future -- this is the meaning of the word womb -- and the main reason for every life is to insure the future of all life . . . by confirming the safe nature of now. Life exists in now; it persists in the future . . . women are the agents of that persistence. Now is the time; today is the day; there has never been a moment that is as opportune as this . . . this is as it is. With life allowed to exist and persist, there stands a chance of enlightenment for every soul . . . the purpose of every soul. Our prayer is with all women of this world, and all the women to be in this world; our prayer is that they are held in the highest regard, and allowed to experience their true nature; allowed to realize their body is a gift from 'Forever' to this exact moment on Earth, and that each woman is given the freedom to govern her own conscious decisions. Peace be with you dear and sacred women of the world.

A massive number of newly born soul-bodies, desperate for evolutionary wisdom, have arrived here on Earth . . . you are one of the wisdom keepers. When you are clear, the present moment is clear, and there is an overriding sensation that future present moments will unfold clearly . . . this is the environment in which these curious and hungry soul-bodies thrive. This world is a product of wise, human, conscious, awareness mixed in with the nature of nature, but thus far, the human part of this equation has been unguided and haphazard. You're on Earth to correct this . . . pratyahar (Sanskrit) is the state of this awareness to synchronize the small parts to the whole . . . connecting the finite to the Infinite. Our prayer is that you are cordial to these newly arrived guests; that you are constantly perceiving the connections within every disconnection; that you become one of the guiding stars to light their path on Earth with a brilliant future, and know that this future is now.

The Earth is currently in a rare moment, not a completely unique one, but clearly a conspicuous moment in the history of human awareness. You have global displays of violence, and reactive governance based in fear. It mimics levels witnessed in all the horrendous periods of history. When human popularity is based on the cruelty of reaction; where the human mind acts without access to empathy, understanding, or compassion it becomes dangerous to life. Human beings have elevated capacities of intelligence and innovation and without the commandments of love, compassion and empathy these innovations of intelligence are always weaponized. Fear and insecurity become the guidance and the governance, extreme individualism becomes the popularity driver, barbarism and intolerance pose as success, and the system honors intolerance beyond all else. These are the roots of the most violent and destructive qualities in the human character. This opportunistic popularity is showing up again today. Intelligence is being measured in the threats of aggression, might is being determined as the right and the authority, and compassion and understanding are seen as weaknesses. In these moments throughout history, living systems are ignorantly devastated. The current extinction rate is one thousand times higher than any previous recording . . . this is billions of years of recorded history. This moment has appeared with every barbaric civilization throughout the true history of this Universe, not the history that's depicted in ever shortened memories of time, but the deeper knowledge that's hidden by fake histories rewritten with the blood-ink of violence and victory all masking the truer legacy. You're facing this false legacy again -- not to fall for its seduction -- but to remember its folly and be the hope. Our prayer is that you climb out of the collective human fog; open your awareness to history -- recent and ancient -- in which this moment has repeated; guarantee that you do not participate in its false images and faulty promises . . . be the hope humanity has hoped for . . . be hopeful in your motivation, and imagine hopeful solutions.

The fabric of spacetime stretches -- spiraling in elliptical bubbles -- throughout the seemingly endless post-etheric space. This is the environment that astronomers and astrophysicists proudly strive to measure with their "yards-stick" like instruments of telescopes; space-telescopes; electron-telescopes, and graviton-telescopes. But nothing, that astronomy, or astrophysics has, can get anywhere close to the caliber of an instrument that would be required to measure the nature of this fabric -- for this fabric stretches into dimensions and materials that have never been known. You cannot measure what you do not know -- you can only measure what can be projected from what has already been . . . beyond that, everything is immeasurable by your standards. In order to imagine that which has never been known, you must imagine when you yourself haven't been known . . . understand when you have been nothing . . . in between your existence periods. In that nothingness, you must be willing to accept explanations that explain nothing . . . nothing that you are aware of that is. When you relax within these explanations -- without the need to jump to the conclusion of -- "this makes no sense" -- then you're on the threshold of discovering the unknown, in the uncharted, within the unfathomable. At the furthest edge of this "territory" . . . within this fully stretched imagination . . . you will have perhaps found a single faint 'minute' thread in the fabric of spacetime, the fabric that spirals on the surface of your own elliptical bubble of a Universe within the massive megaverse, within the boundless multiverse. This is the bubble that is not perceivable with any of the "yardstick" like instruments your scientists so proudly use . . . you see, the key to measuring that far out there, is not out there at all . . . it's within you. Our prayer is that you are fully surrendered to measuring the furthest reaches of all possibilities by knowing it in yourself; that you reduce the two-dimensional polarities that constantly tell you there are limits, and expand your Universe to include that which does not yet exist.

In order to make a strong move in the material world, you either have to believe in it; be inspired by it; be tricked into moving it, or be forced into the move. Because of the barbaric nature of today's psycho-emotional atmosphere, the most admired and acquired skills, are the clever skills that can trick a person -- or the power skills that can force a person into movement. Both of these skills are highly paid for; very unnatural; emotional depleting, and harmful to the body. However, this is the current unnatural nature of human nature, and out of this comes the many challenges of disease and unrest that you're currently experiencing. These times have been forewarned -- in the ancient wisdom scriptures it says: "In the Kali Yug . . . the darkest time . . . truth will be that which convinces." That did not say truth would be true. In other words, this is the time when facts do not make up truths, but are simply used as mechanisms to convince and force movement. These times are abusive to the body, the emotions and the mind . . . the only healing is found in your heart. And even though the brain feels safer, and the heart feels vulnerable -- the heart is the sanctuary . . . it's accessed through the doors of your courage. These are the times that require that courage -- it comes through deep breathing; long walks; stronger bonds with wives, husbands, partners, lovers, children, pets, and friends; more yoga and meditation, music, art and fun . . . all to balance out that psychic corruption. These activities will lead you to the moment that's right here . . . right now, and the benefits of 'now' are immeasurable . . . because 'now' has not yet been corrupted. Our prayer is that you recognize the times are what they are; gather with those who are not being fooled by the corruption of these times, and are not submitting to the false pressures of that corruption; keep yourself energized with the sacred pure calmness of 'now' at all moments, and always practice being brutally honest . . . always with a smile.

There are many forms of yoga, meditation and spiritual practice. Often, these practices recommend not eating the trinity roots -- onion, garlic and ginger -- because these foods are considered too tamasic (emotionally and sexually stimulating). When the purpose of a spiritual practice is to elevate life beyond the emotions, being emotionally and sexually stimulated can be counterproductive. The kundalini energy is the energy of your higher awareness; it's naturally dormant and rests at the dant'ian point, a physical nerve center in the middle of the lower abdomen -- the same region that contains these emotional and sexual energies. In kundalini yoga and meditation, there are specific purposes for stimulating this area. It not only awakens these emotional energies but it also awakens the dormant kundalini. When the energy of the kundalini uncoils under this stimulation, it moves from the lower centers to the heart center and then from the heart center into the higher centers of awareness. The trinity roots can play a key role. They energize the base, stimulate the sexual and emotional energy and then stabilize and align the preliminary channel. The key is discipline. With proper discipline, this sexual/emotional energy transmutes into spiritual energy. It can be used in everything from sublime sex to being sublimely enlightened. The nature of a kundalini practice is not only to become sublimely enlightened, but also to be fully involved in the world as an "enlightened householder." The difference between these roles – 'worldly' and 'spiritual' -- are merely angles of perception. Like the emotions of fear and excitement, they are the exact same sensations with simple shifts in the angle of perception. Excitement looks toward hope and fear looks away from hope. By stimulating and raising the kundalini, you master these angles by not only finding hope but also transmuting your fears into excitement and then excitement into inspiration. Our prayer is that you discipline your emotional energies and shift their angles of perception into experiencing your highest experience . . . this is being alive . . . practice being alive.

There's a Dragonfly with an English common name of "wandering glider" and "globe skimmer" -- referring to its migratory behavior -- it's the new insect migration record holder. It travels over 11,000 miles while looking for suitable pools to lay its eggs and mate with one another. This is nearly twice the distance covered by the previous record holder, the Monarch butterfly, which flies up to 6,000 miles. To do this, the Dragonflies fly at altitudes of over 20,000 feet, feeding on aerial plankton along the way; travelling all this distance without ever landing. At this elevation there are winds that keep them aloft and carry them forward with their wings acting like sails . . . this is a world created by nature for the preservation of this specie . . . every need provided for. This particular Dragonfly is now found all over the world -- from high in the Himalayas, to Easter Island in the South Pacific. This little creature does not arrive at its destination exhausted -- it arrives energetic and ready -- having rode these winds to fulfill its destiny. In your world of accomplishment achieved through great effort, this represents the elegance of an alternative . . . of how surrender can be the greater path of accomplishing your goals. Whether you refer to it as surrender to GOD, or science, or Cosmos, or the force of nature . . . the name doesn't matter, surrendering to that which will carry you forward is quite contrary to the current human will. But when you study a creature such as this, you can observe how surrendering to the winds of life will carry you to your fulfillment. This is what happens when any creature trusts GOD, nature, the Universe and Destiny. Our prayer is that you set your sails to ride the winds of your imagination; trust yourself into the hands of nature which only desires your fulfillment; allow these winds to carry you to your destination and arrive refreshed, rewarded and fulfilled.

In the vast human apparatus of perception it is good to remember that the details we observe through our senses are not the facts, they are our interpretations of the facts. When our meditative mind brings us into a place of silence, we are more able to perceive fact over interpretation. Our prayer is that you find silence often.

*A*rchaeology has explored the similarities in ancient arti-
facts from geographically diverse regions. The Mayans,
Egyptians and Sumerians each used similar symbols all clearly
depicting space "aliens." One theory is that highly advanced
extraterrestrials seeded human life on Earth in these areas.
Intriguing and compelling analysis has gone into such theories.
It adds great value and adds richness to the human story. There
are other explanations as well. Hundreds of miles below the surface of the Earth there exists the records of previous Earthly
realities buried under the massive collisions of constantly shifting tectonic plates. There's no way of knowing the exact age or
history of this planet because the accumulation of these shifts
has renewed the Earth's surface over and over, just like the skin
on your body renews every few months. Similarly, the shifting gravitational waves of this megaverse creates many different
'celestial' constellations over millions of years in the larger time.
Within all this shifting and renewal lie countless opportunities
for many histories and other explanations of this ancient art. In
the yogic mythologies, the Vedic records, there are versions of
history based on the model that you are currently living as the
'fifth evolution of the human race' . . . four previous humani-
ties existed here on Earth. People, very similar to you, evolved
the abilities of space-travel . . . only to self-destruct from mis-
handling their technology. At the most advanced stages, these
ancient civilizations created temporary homes in the Arctic
regions, here they practiced 'out of body' celestial travel and
advanced enlightenment using the power of Earth's magnetic

poles. This Arctic home is written about in the Vedas; in Santa Claus' flying sleigh -- and the Scandinavian and Estonian languages contain remnants of Sanskrit from these migrations passing through their region. Our prayer is that you are open to exploring the endless possibilities of history; that you believe in magic as well as logic, and love, and allow your life to become an outstanding future . . . and be extraordinary, right now.

There's an old saying, "Tis better to give than to receive." Yogis and spiritual masters realized the opposite to be true quite long ago . . . they realized that nature can't give anything without first receiving. Therefore, it's only possible to receive -- and then give. Anything that's given, that hasn't first been received, has been stolen. Receiving is the initial step; it's the way of the heart . . . you give when you've received to the point of overflowing. It's not only material, it's also overflowing with love that carries material with it . . . this is nature's abundance and the way of service. When your cup overflows, there's no sense of actually giving -- you're just abundant, and grateful, and full, and flowing over. This is also the quantum law of the material Universe . . . the true nature of prosperity . . . everything is everywhere and endlessly occurring always. When this is truly your relationship with matter -- when you're receiving and you do not feel indebted -- when you're giving and you're not taking credit; you're not keeping score; you're not holding debt . . . this is love. When life is experienced at this level -- it's experienced as ease, joy, knowing, and complete freedom . . . this is that "overflowing-cup." In order to experience life at this level of love: deeply embrace your highest value, naturally; consume any negativity as pure fuel . . . no other interpretations; believe mistakes are the pathway to getting it right, and do what you don't know how to do. Children have these qualities -- it's the way they learn and grow. Fear has to be taught to them -- it's thought to be safe, but this form of safety is dangerous -- it doesn't learn; it doesn't grow; it doesn't teach, or overflow. Our prayer is that you make all the mistakes you can and love them; work through their lessons quickly and grow beyond them to the point of being full; receive this fullness without indebtedness . . . whatever negativity you encounter along the way, just think of it as fuel for the path to overflowing. Be a master who benefits everyone without keeping score . . . receive and overflow.

*O*bjective studies have shown that wolves have over two thousand different howls, with the differences being in tone, pitch, intensity and fluctuation. Domesticated dogs have these same differences in their barks. The conclusion is that the words, in the animal world, are tonal words, not words made up of syllables differentiated by letters. This same study could be down throughout the animal kingdom and find that all creatures have complex language and communicate extensively. They've found that horses recognize your facial expression . . . the angle of your head and body. This is also the way they communicate with each other. When humans think of animals as less intelligent than themselves, it's not a measure of intelligence it's a judgement of misunderstanding. When you think about it, it's actually humans who lack the intelligence to perceive the intelligence of animals . . . you even do this with each other. That's because human intelligence tends to be exclusive and competitive rather than inclusive; to think of exceptionality rather than commonality -- it is this same attitude that pits one group of humans against another. Nature does not participate in this; when there's a herd, or a flock mentality amongst other species, it's not about ideology, but for procreation and their life order. The human exceptionalism creates death by war; justifies ruthless violence; eliminates compassion and opens conflicts around the world. It allows the slaughter of so many animals on a daily basis that this industry is the number one cause of atmospheric oxygen loss. There was even a time when humans did not consider that other animals have a soul . . . still prevalent today . . .

another obvious lack of intelligence on our part. When you get right down to it, humans are the only animal on Earth that is globally disruptive . . . that's not at all intelligent. Our prayer is that you see yourself in all others; discover the unique intelligence in all creatures; adjust your diet to be a friend to life, and allow all life to prosper.

*H*uman evolution has placed sentries at the gate of experience in order to shield out unwanted sensations. With this shielding we are unable to experience our experiences so we think about and analyze them instead and live in a world of brain noise. Our prayer is that you call upon your sentries to stand down and give yourself the experience of your life . . . in mental silence.

*H*umans and pre-humans began speaking very early in their development. All creatures have some form of language, but since we're not privy to its actual nature, we've often discounted its complexity and accuracy. We've defined languages, other than our own, as primitive, but that's our ignorance, for we're now learning that many complexities exist in the languages of animals and also plants . . . complexities we're not even close to understanding. Computer algorithms have discovered over two thousand varieties of 'howling' in wolves -- there are variations within each of these . . . wolves are communicating over two thousand unique messages. Human vocal anatomy is extremely complex . . . you're the only animal that's currently defined as forming a consonant . . . all creatures form vowels. Vowels produce the sound and consonants direct that sound throughout the body and outside the body. This is the basis of the science of mantra. The word 'language' is the compression of two very old words -- langue & guage . . . the gauge or measuring of the length or depth with the tongue. Language allows you to measure the depth of any moment through descriptions using your words. It's your right to make up words, but very few people exercise this right . . . all words were made up at some point. A great word -- one that was coined by Robert Heinlein in Stranger in a Strange Land 'grok' . . . meaning to absolutely and fully comprehend the details of a moment. Yogi Bhajan invented a word -- it's Humanology; it describes the science of being human that accompanies the practice of a strong, disciplined, spiritual technology. You have every right to use language like you own it. Our prayer is that you have the audacity to exercise this right and speak your mind; to build words that work for you in your world; teach these words to others and use them freely; use all words like they're your friends, for they define the life within you and around you; build relations with your language and discover reasons to speak from your heart. Then, when it's your moment to be silent, enjoy the silence without a single word.

*M*aking mistakes is a sign of growth; of trying something brand new, or so unusual that you don't recognize it. There can never be growth without trying something new -- there cannot be growth without mistakes. Making mistakes is rewarded by nature, it's the elimination of possibilities on the road to accomplishment. Evolution has been deeply studied; it attempts up to fifty thousand different efforts before it finds one that causes growth, survival, progress and prosperity. Scientists, studying this phenomenon of evolution, have marveled at the absolute forgiveness within nature . . . this is the forgiveness that allows the failures to learn, rather than experience guilt in failure . . . guilt shuts down curiosity . . . curiosity is essential to growth. In the schools now, children must be rewarded for all efforts -- the ones that are totally correct, and the ones that are wrong. There can be no scholastic competitions -- because life, at the level of the current evolution, is not a comparison -- it's an expression . . . every expression is unique like the print of the fingers, and the pattern of the iris. This will begin to educate children toward peace . . . the peace required for human life on Earth to survive. We've reached the point in our evolutionary progress where there are no longer any threats except the ones that humans are creating themselves. Once reaching this point -- on any planet -- the life-system has only a limited number of generations to turn all its efforts into benevolent ones. Without this shift away from the self-induced crisis -- the crisis will evolve faster than survival -- the system will implode and self-destruct . . . that's the nature of evolution. Either peace evolves, or violence evolves, whichever is made more important. Our prayer is that you make all the mistakes that are required for you to grow with the peace in your heart; that you educate your children to be compassionate not competitive; that you reward their mistakes so that they love their curiosity . . . and with this love they will build their prosperous world.

*I*0,000 years ago survival was transformed with the cultivation of seeds and the introduction of farming. When evolution advances through a sublimation point (sublimation like when water turns into steam), so much changes that very little remains familiar . . . unfamiliarity breeds fear. A previous sublimation was when we stood up on two legs and began relying on our balance. Cultivating seeds was as profound as standing up -- it altered the way the brain works -- humans changed from hunters to cultivators. The challenge today is that many on Earth have shifted into cultivator mode, but the world is still dominated by the hunters . . . who are still hunting. These hunters dominate politics, business, religion and life -- fixated on the "enemy" -- they're never at peace. They require civilization to develop more advanced weapons, but they do not cultivate the compassion required to actually advance civilization. In the hunter's mind, any other being is a potential threat -- in the cultivator's mind any other being is a potential helper. With "hunters" dominating civilization, it's not civilized -- everyone is a potential threat. Not everyone is hunting, but everyone is influenced, or affected by the "hunt" . . . it ignores the elderly and their wisdom; it ignores the young and their education; it loses touch with the prosperity of life, and focuses all available resources on the "hunt." This promotes corruption as an "asset" in the struggle . . . you're not considered smart, unless you're aggressively smart; you're not considered successful, unless you've conquered all "enemies" to get there. Another demonstration of this "hunter" corruption: in a world with plenty of food and transportation -- 30,000 people (mostly children under the age of five) starve to death every day . . . only hunters would allow this. Our prayer is that you practice each day to eliminate your hunting mind; restore the cultivating mind that cultivates compassion, and tend to the crops of life on a planet that's itself alive. Teach each other to relate in this way, and cultivate the culture of a civilization that's civilized.

*I*nfinity is beyond your imagination -- what appears to be infinite is only an idea. To imagine, or perceive anything, it must have some definition and definition is a boundary . . . infinity cannot have boundaries. There's a familiar law of the physical Universe: "for every action there's an equal reaction." Whatever action is present, the equal reaction must also be present. This cannot be limited -- within each moment there's every possible question . . . therefore, every possible solution is there. This appears to be infinity, and since you cannot imagine infinity, you have difficulty imagining that every solution must be there. The ancient masters would say: "Within each breath are the keys to the moment; the solutions to the problem; the answers to the question." Since there's no limit to the questions in any moment, there can be no limit to the answers. However, in order to discover these answers, and solutions, and keys -- which are the reactions to the actions of the problems, questions, and dilemmas -- you must also be present in your breath. Being present in the breath does not mean just physically breathing -- it means being in your 'presence' -- in the 'presence' of your breath. You obtain and maintain this presence by drawing each breath in a conscious and affirmative way . . . fully sensing and being 'mindful' of your action. With this presence, comes the answers and solutions . . . but not only to the challenges that you already have -- also to the challenges you might imagine having. In other words . . . when you imagine your most perfect dream scenario . . . every challenge that could block this dream will also appear. Action -- reaction . . . consciously breathe your imagined dream, and you breathe the challenges and their solutions as well. Our prayer is that you practice this opportunity; be your "infinite" nature within the nature of every breath you take; open to the answers and the answers will open to you . . . that's the law . . . live your dream.

*G*etting in touch with and reveling in the character of your character, your basic cosmic self, is the reason for existence and the path to good health, abundant happiness and spiritual fulfillment. Our prayer is that you find your path and walk it daily toward this prosperity.

*A*ncient mastery is being rediscovered -- the material Universe is a network of inseparable patterns and relationships that are all alive and communicating with light, sound, movement and pure energy. It's also becoming obvious that this is not simple mechanics -- this has a real life force -- it's a complete system of living organisms. Most of this scale is so huge that it's unable to be seen as a single organism, but even eco-science now recognizes Earth is a living being . . . Gaia with a consciousness. Masters and indigenous people throughout the ages understood this; honored this; taught this, and practiced this. The polarity -- the barbaric view, where the Earth and Cosmos are just mechanical, like a clockwork -- has only been believed for the past thousand years -- and only within a small portion of the planet. But now this attitude has spread like a virus, first with colonization, and now with global economics. Advanced astroscience has realized that planets; stars; all celestial systems are the cells and organs of much grander living, cognitive entities . . . exactly like the ancient and indigenous knowledge. Recognition that this complexity and nonlinear patterns are the life of vast organisms stretching across the Universe is an epiphany that holds keys for solving many current issues. Society and social justice; health and healing; education; human rights; political systems; environments and economics -- when everything is a part of a living system, life becomes solvable. The evolution of "obvious" life did not begin with the first "obvious' living cell, it began billions of years earlier with a process of 'prebiotics' . . . the evolution of this entire living multiverse. Our prayer is that you recognize life and consciousness in everything around you; that you honor these living entities as parts in the much larger life; that you derive great emotional energy from all of these relations, just as you would from any person or animal, and teach this to the adults and children of the world . . . it will ultimately reveal the peace and great harmony that is the core of all life.

*A*s your current opportunity of achieving mastery convenes with the certainty of global disruption, you are left to participate in an ironic marriage of odd partners. In the years to come the global leadership will be requesting guidance from spiritual masters . . . the times will require it and it's the currency of our basic structure. Our prayer is that you see yourself authorized for this important role and deliver the guidance with humility and grace.

*E*volution is incredibly compassionate: there's a fungi growing just inches under the surface of the world's forests -- it's the largest individual mass of any organism on Earth. One that's been discovered covers two thousand acres in the old-growth forest of Oregon State. Mycelium, as it's called, has evolved into the neurological network of nature -- creating systems of phenomenal information sharing for life of all kinds. It has ecological awareness; reacts to changes in climate, and collectively maintains the long-term health of its environment through constant communication and complex responses. The basic science is: Microscopic cells called "mycelium" -- the fruit of which are mushrooms -- work to recycle the carbon, the nitrogen, and many other essential elements, as they break down plant and animal debris to create rich new soil. Over the millions of years, other abilities emerged from this system as evolution continued to nurture the plant-kingdom. Young trees, in the middle of tall forests, were unable to grow because of the lack of sunlight in the vast denseness. Mycelium learned to transfer the nutrients of sunlight from the meadows, where it's abundant, to the baby trees in the middle of the dark forest . . . the "babies" thrived. These networks have expanded to cover every forest on Earth. This mycelium communication serves as an example of the systemic networks that are desperately needed for the future of the dense, diverse "forest" of humanity. Animals are more closely related to this fungi than to any other kingdom -- more than 600 million years ago there was a shared ancestry. This represents the new evolution -- it has arrived on Earth right now.

Because you're reading this, it shows you're one of the curious, compassionate, sage/warriors who will create this new evolution for humanity to thrive. Our prayer is that you maintain your curiosity; that you take the lead in creating these networks of compassionate communication, and then discover the countless ways you can help 'life' that's in such need. If it takes someone to step up, why not you . . . if it needs to happen sometime soon, why not now?

_T_he material Universe is so immeasurably vast that there's no means for the human brain to fathom the distances, or the times, involved in its measureless measure. Within this, your life is both significant and insignificant at the same moment; there's nothing lost in this vastness, and yet there's nothing that's completely known. In all this immensity, the one sensation that every human has to discover, in order to advance to their full potential, is inclusion -- the capacity to perceive the "other" as a part of the 'self'. And this inclusion is to apply universally -- it's to be the same for everything, everywhere. This is a prerequisite for you to advance toward compassionate living and true fulfillment. Let's be honest here, it's easy to include those who are closest -- this is the, "I am you and you are me routine." But how do you include everyone and everything? It's very difficult to include your enemies; to include the most despicable parts of this world -- or the most distant pieces. It's confusing to think that all these parts are still you, but there's an easier view that can get you started. Think of a photograph, the greater the clarity in the detail of a photograph is in the greater number of pixels it has . . . the more tiny dots per square inch (PSI). Also note that in order for the details of a photo to make sense, there has to be light, and shadow, and lines of distinction. Now view those parts of your world, that are extremely unpleasant, as simply the dots -- within the millions of dots (the PSI) -- that compose the shadows and lines in your total photograph . . . without them, there's no measure, or depth in it. They make you distinct; they make you visible as you; without their inclusion in your world, there's no way for you to be fully recognized as you. This is the nature of reality; this is the reality of compassion; this is the meaning of inclusion. Our prayer is that you include everyone and everything in the picture of your "self"; include them as they are -- with all their faults and flaws -- they are just pixels in your total picture. They allow your world to be richer in its depth and detail . . . this is the compassionate view.

The Sun and its gravitationally held system of planets flies through our galaxy at 43,000 miles per hour, while the Milky Way itself moves through the universe at a phenomenal 1.3 million miles per hour. Within all of this massive movement, the light from your body radiates outward at the speed of 670 million miles per hour. Our prayer is that you realize -- recognizing and using your power, within this massive multiverse, is the greatest gift you can give back to GOD who gave you the greatest gift of all . . . your life and its light.

*S*ailing the winds of enthusiasm and inspiration are as close to total freedom as you can get in a physical body . . . all that's required are the sails of believing. To the contrary -- doubt is extremely costly -- it will cost you your momentum; your belief; your faith, and your energy in any moment. Every day doubt struggles against the winds and ultimately loses touch with your dreams. The paths of enthusiasm and inspiration are neither logical, nor reasonable . . . you must simply believe you have the authority . . . that's that. Claiming this authority is always questioned by doubt -- this is why the true value of enthusiasm and inspiration has to be unreasonable . . . claim them both without any "arguable" reason. When logical doubt faces off against this unreasonable inspiration and enthusiasm -- there's no contest -- the advantage is always on the side without reasons . . . there are no handles to hold and divert the energy. It takes on the appearance of great courage and focus, yet it's gentle and simply "from the heart." This is the exact nature of nature; this is how everything in this Universe has evolved through the eons of time. It all evolved against tremendous odds within innumerable doubts. It's the survival of the most fit, and the ones that fit together most agreeably have always prevailed. Strength and fitness are achieved by lifting against the opposing forces. Overcoming opposition without reasons says you deserve to be equal to the moment; gives you momentum and traction to experience clarity in the midst of chaos . . . this is evolution . . . this is in fact the Cosmic reality . . . this is the Universal law. It's this equality that allows 'time' to do the heavy lifting, while inspired enthusiasm makes the decisions of direction through 'space'. Our prayer is that you take huge advantage of this natural law; allow it to unfold your authority to be unreasonably enthusiastic with every single day; to face your gains and losses with unreasonable inspiration and choose your own direction . . . allow your inherent freedom to do the rest.

*T*he emotional, mental and physical aspects of life have unique cycles. These cycles are: the 7 year cycle of the emotional body; the 11 year cycle of the mental body; the 18 year cycle of the physical body. There are also certain times in life when the end/beginning moments of these periods nearly coincide with one another -- when two or three of these cycles form periods of combined influence. These are known as proportional clusters. An example is when the 18 year cycle of your physical body -- occurs near the 21 year (3x7) cycle of your emotional body -- occurring right next to the 22 years (2x11) cycle of the mental body. Charting these cycles and clusters reveals a map of life's influences. Life is not happenchance -- it's a chartable opportunity that unfolds under predictable influences. Knowing this puts important science into the art of living. When you use this measurable and predictable nature of science -- in combination with the creative and joyful style of art -- you have an accurate and joyful life. (Some practical references of these cycles) The 7 year cycle of the emotional body has been referred to as: "The seven year itch" and "Break a mirror -- you get seven years bad luck." The 11 year cycle of the mental body is identical to the 11 year cycle of the Sun's solar storms . . . light photons (that feed the pineal gland in the brain) storming toward Earth. The 18 year cycle of your physical body refers to -- all the cells of your body are known to be replaced every eighteen years . . . you are never older than 18, except for your memories. This is why it is so vital for you to recapitulate your memories through meditation . . . hold the great ones close to your heart, and release painful charges from bad ones . . . bad memories without this charge are instructive lessons. Our prayer is that you honor all your bodies: feed your physical body with great nutrition, exercise and rest; feed your emotional body with effective and cleansing meditation -- reshaping your responses to the moments of life; feed your mental body with the discipline of constructive thinking (mindfulness) . . . do this with both the science of knowledge, and the art of joy.

The Bhavishya Purana, one of the eighteen Puranas, is the future tales of ancient times. It's a work that contains prophecies regarding today, written thousands of years ago, and a few legends that have actually taken place in history. Our prayer is that you pay close attention to all that's happening and then view everything within the largest context you can imagine . . . this will begin to let you understand the subtle connections everywhere.

Within every culture, on every continent, throughout the history that is known and the pre-history that's only slightly known, one of the most common of all mythologies has been the stories of Dragons. These stories are so common in these annals that it's clear -- Dragons once existed in a time that's been buried from any means of proving that they ever existed -- the mythologies that still remember and repeat these stories are true. This is the way it is with such things . . . only known to that which is unknown. In the East, the tales were of Dragons being sacred, and of taming and using these Dragons for the benefit of life. In the West, where the cultures were always more aggressive and barbaric, their mythologies were of slaying and conquering the Dragons for the safety of life. It's important to understand the differences within these differences. In the East, the Dragon was understood as the representative of the five elements -- earth, water, fire, air and ether -- they were the earth in that they were physical; they were water with their webbed feet; they were fire with what they were breathing; they were air in that they could fly, and they were the ether because they were such mystical beings. The idea in the East has always been -- when you tame the five elements, you understand them, and then use them . . . Dragons, when you ride them, make for great transportation. In the West, where life has always been based in fear of survival and the unknown -- anything that was more powerful could never be tamed -- it always needed to be conquered. That's the nature of barbarism, and has always been. The name George was from the word 'geo' which means 'Earth'

(the planet) . . . George was the Dragon slayer. The mystical threats of the Cosmos -- are not to be understood and used -- but are to be destroyed by the Earthly powers. What a waste of really good magic, and great transportation. Our prayer is that you tame all of your Dragons; ride them with their magical powers throughout all of your dreams, and find them to be the greatest way to get from place to place, while connecting all your dots. Dragons will help with your greatest successes.

*A*ll that's lost simply exists in a new location and often the search to find it walks you through moments of your life that you might otherwise be unwilling to walk through. You can set a course to lose and release all that holds you back, then coordinate your observation to find its new location and condition . . . one that moves you forward toward your destiny -- your desires. Extend this principle to the full extent that you want, for within this material universe, within the multi-verse, nothing can be lost or destroyed -- only transformed -- and this cosmic model is a map toward a more perfect outcome, a sense of purpose, and a connection to source. Our prayer is that you discover the new locations of all your lost dreams and follow their map toward the core of the purpose of your life.

*M*usic is the mathematics of sound; equations are the harmonics that promote healing and success . . . physical, emotional, and psychological. Together with the lyrics of your life -- the poems that evolve through the expressions of your heart and mind -- these combinations form the songs that accompany your life. Riding the intersection of these waves -- the lyrics and sounds . . . the poems and harmonies -- you exist in the music amongst them. Some passages of life are in total harmony, while others are in complete disarray . . . when you authentically live within your own version, you experience freedom. This is the freedom affecting all your choices -- free to decide, in every moment, if you're going for success, or looking for an excuse. Subconsciously, every human knows that success may bring the rejection of jealousy -- and an excuse will often bring sympathy. There's music imbedded in each of these events. The music of jealousy is that you're rejected for your great value; the music of sympathy is that you're not rejected, but you're living with an excuse. There's jealousy and rejection on every road of success -- around every revelation, or innovation -- this is the music of nature, "for every action there's an equal reaction." One of the most common reasons to avoid success and look for an excuse is to avoid this rejection and receive that sympathy. Humans are the only creatures rewarded with sympathy -- all other creatures in nature, when needing an excuse, will often perish. Humans use the "sweetness" of sympathy to demonstrate caring, and ultimately compassion, but it needs to be used sparingly, otherwise it replaces success. Our prayer is that even when you're surrounded by jealousy and rejection; even when the tensions of chaotic melodies are attacking you; even when that "sweet" sympathy is waiting for your excuse -- even then -- you sing out the song of your success . . . the one that's been playing in your heart since the day you were born . . . the one that's always singing in your head, with all those unusual harmonies, and the true sweetness and freedom of success.

*O*ur bodies are filled with nano-crystal-catalysts and intel-likeys . . . the magical elements at our command within the logical natures of our human bio-system. Our prayer is that you tune into these magical parts and learn how to take full advantage of their logic.

There are winds of plasma, in the distances between galaxies, where nothing seems to exist . . . they travel at nearly 400 thousand miles per hour. And these aren't even the fastest winds in the Universe -- NASA's Chandra X-ray Observatory has found faster winds in the stellar-masses of black holes -- winds racing through space at over 20 million miles per hour. These distant winds are impacting the Earth and your life, even though there's no direct contact. They've produced major changes across the ages of humankind . . . truly the winds of change. The momentum and torque of these winds distorts and bends the space and time -- and even without any direct contact, and over such vast distances, this bending and distortion has an effect on this solar system and how its space and time are perceived. Space-bending alters perception over vast periods -- like a gigantic lens of time, or the shifts in the seasons -- and the only way these results can be measured is through the deep historical references recorded in mythology . . . the mythology that's true. The ages known as yugas are one example of this record, as is the intersection between the science of astronomy (the placement, movement and location of celestial events) -- and astrology (the effects these events have on your psycho-emotional and physical world). There's so much that's misunderstood about massive space and most people have no idea about time . . . you call it an illusion. Science is completely mistaken about the age and origin of this Universe; about the parallels to space, and your coexistence in alternate times. It's as if science still believes in a "flat-Earth." Our prayer is that you're enormously curious;

that your curiosity drives a constant discovery; that each discovery alters your perception and beliefs, and you allow the winds of change to produce new realities . . . which will also need to change. This is the path of awareness and growth -- this growth and awareness creates acceptance; this acceptance ultimately produces understanding, and it's this understanding that brings about a lasting peace.

*L*ife unfolds as time in space -- each moment registers an impression in the brain, the body and the aura (the electromagnetic field around you). Each event impresses each moment, and then the next . . . and so on. When the impression of any moment is held into the next moment, it's a memory. When a memory influences the moment, it's called learning. This is good, but when memory is too strong, you experience a distortion of the moment. As the system accumulates memory, unless properly processed -- these layers will eventually overwhelm the present . . . you're no longer living in the moment. In fact, you're not living at all, you're remembering and reacting. Another gift for learning from human evolution -- in addition to your own memories -- your body's epigenetics contains memories from seven generations past -- that's 254 ancestors adding to this moment . . . their knowledge; their emotions; their aspirations. To actually experience a moment as what it is -- inside this much influence -- you require the discipline of meditation to clarify the mind, and yoga to deeply process the body's epigenetics. Look around this world -- people are interacting in so many ways -- some in business; in politics; in religion, and everyone just in daily life. Evolution taught humans to memorize; this gave you great progress, but evolution hasn't taught you yet how to clear this memory; how to live in the moment; to experience the 'what is' and the magnificent presence that's always present. Like driving without paying attention -- there's an emotional accident taking place in today's human interactions. This is human nature . . . it's up to you to find your way back to this moment's nature. Forgiveness is the healthiest way to process the chaos and experience your present moment. Our prayer is that you have the strength, or find the strength, or create the strength to have a disciplined daily practice -- one that processes your memory, to then live in the present moment; to learn from the past, but not live in it -- forgive and be nourished by the experience of 'what is' in the present moment . . . and grow into a magnificent future.

Studies by our good friend, the late Jonathon Lilly, demonstrated that Dolphins have the healthiest emotional body of any mammal. They will always be honest and authentic; completely exposing their true feelings, for a maximum of fifteen seconds, and then they're over it. Whether it's anger, joy, jealousy, sadness, or any other emotion, they don't hold it in. Humans nuance their emotions, they hold on to them, they build up inside the body where they stagnate and corrupt the current moment with the pent up emotional messaging of previous moments. It was the Buddha who said, "Any emotion, when fully experienced or expressed, turns into joy." This is because 'joy' is the foundation of all emotions . . . the base coat in the emotional body. Without this ability to fully release your emotions into the moment from which they arise, they linger and ambush future moments -- in which they may not apply, may not be welcome -- but come out when you're least prepared. After a time, these "armies" of emotions, roaming in the background of your psyche, build their opportunities to launch an attack . . . not because they're bad or plotting, but because they're biologically stored in the tissue of your body, and must be released. Not only is it unhealthy to hold them in, it's actually impossible. This is one of the reasons why a daily practice of meditation and yoga are so beneficial. In these practices you're able to process these stored emotions and move them through the body without having to "target" someone or something with them. Processing emotions through physical postures and meditation is not only healthy -- it's extremely revealing . . .

you learn about yourself and the deeper layers of your experiences. Our prayer is that you experience your emotions with the authenticity of expression -- internal and external; that you process the ones that are unexpressed through your daily practice; that you live each moment -- unencumbered by any debris from the past, and experience this clarity in the joy of authenticity and honesty.

*E*nter into each and every moment with the complete and total knowing of your equality and that which makes you equal to the moment will come to you. It arrives as an inspiration, an idea, and a thought in the form of a solution and or answer. Our prayer is that you are always equal to this task.

*T*he fragrance of your life's purpose permeates the heart; your tongue is intuitively attracted to the taste of it. The French word for living in the heart is 'courage'. The tongue is an actual extension of the fascia surrounding the heart . . . the tongue connects the heart to the outside. This is why we speak with, taste the flavors of life with, and kiss with it . . . each are sensations from the heart. The mind is deeply satisfied by meditating on these sensations; the body finds the ease of good health in them. Such are the pure musings of the 'imaginal cells' -- ideas deep inside the chrysalis of your heart's projection and prayer. These 'cells' are imaginative seeds of your future potential; they contain a blueprint of the most perfect you, living beyond any limits found in your current world. Each one of these 'cells' operates independently as an individual seed, an idea within this purpose -- like a single-cell organism. Sometimes your attitude will regard these 'imaginal cells' to be invaders, to be threats -- because they are in fact a disruption to the status quo. Like any threat to this "normal," these 'imaginal cells' will be attacked by your emotional 'immune system' of doubts. But if you're blessed -- your imagination will persist -- these 'imaginal cells' will multiply and connect with each other to form clusters that resonate together until they reach a tipping point . . . and then the "butterfly" of your life's purpose emerges from the status quo. Such is the experience of every courageous leader, born out of challenge to discover new ways to meet the challenge, and then work with others to transform imagination into reality. Our prayer is that you realize you're

one of these courageous leaders; that you're always transforming with the boundlessness of your own imaginal cells; that you
know deep inside your imagination that you're destined to fulfill your purpose. And each day you find it in your heart -- in
your heartfelt words and actions -- the courage to give a smile,
and get a smile . . . to give a hug, and get a hug . . . the fragrance
of purpose is like a giant game of tag . . . and you're it.

Self-value is the relationship you have to your identity in spacetime . . . that which you are and that which you're not. Through the space you occupy and the space around you . . . the time you've passed through and the time yet to come, the value you place on you is reflected back to you with every breath you take and moment you meet. Yogis have advised for millennia, "Enter the space that's not yet occupied, and then move into the space that does not yet exist." Our prayer is that you constantly value the space you fill and the time you spend, and then experience the limitless freedom of an extraordinary life by creating and developing that which has never ever existed before.

*T*he rhythms of your pulse, push melodies through your blood, vibrating in the arteries and capillaries of your circulation, like the strings on an instrument. Your body plays a song of life . . . resonating constantly inside you, from the moment you're born to the moment of your passing. As distinctive as the prints on each finger, and the iris in your eyes, this melody and rhythm are yours alone . . . unique in every way. The nature of this song -- though completely unique for each individual -- affects everyone exactly the same . . . it uplifts the moment; it clarifies the situation; it satisfies and awakens . . . that is -- if you're listening. It's a tune you can rely on in a pinch, and in the most delightful of moments, to keep you in tune with what's happening. And when you relate to it -- you're elevated over challenges; accepted through restrictions to build a moment into momentum that allows you to rest in peace within your pressures. Every day, your singing blood travels over 19,000 km . . . 12,000 miles, through the more than 60,000 miles of capillaries contained in your body. What a magnificent instrument serenades each one of your thirty to seventy trillion body cells. The music is both a love song and a dance tune . . . it's anything you need, whenever you need it. Any mood can be altered; any moment can be captured; any challenge can be mastered; any mission can be structured, and then delivered . . . all by paying close attention to your song. And that's the key, you must pay attention in order for your life-song to be effective. When your current dream -- the one at the "present" layer of your awareness needs altering -- your life-song navigates through the openings to the light in the labyrinth of the illusion. This is when the commotional charge will raise its voice of doubt, but your song can satisfy the moment . . . listen to it. Our prayer is that you know your song well; that you're listening to it right now as you read these words -- and every day you make certain that you play along with your song.

Since the days in the caves, men have dominated relations with women . . . not because they're better, but because they've been genetically trained to think they're stronger. This genealogical thinking is set up, and it's true, a man is much more physically powerful than a woman, but a woman is up to sixteen times more emotionally powerful than a man. This is used in the bearing and raising the future of everyone, but this is also why there's so much abuse . . . not more today than ever before . . . just more documented. A woman can take a man into emotional realms where he reverts to his physical power . . . the lowest denominator in evolution where he maintains his perceived advantage. It's the natural insecurity within equality . . . there's been no equality for millions of years. A major change to break this outdated pattern -- no matter how hard you will try . . . if you can't see it -- you won't change it. Since it's an all-inclusive environment -- as Einstein would say -- there's no relativity outside the fact . . . the fact remains without challenge. Like the nose on your face, the only way you can actually see it to change it, is with a mirror; in this case the mirror is that which isn't what is. This is the 'speak' of relativity . . . there has to be something that isn't, in order to actually perceive the 'what is'. In this case, that which isn't, is a woman. This is exactly who will lead us out of this violently male dominated world . . . the women are the answer to peace on Earth. You will have to have patience with the process on both sides . . . it's not going away in a generation. The process has to get started however, and in order to start, everyone will have to stop embracing the biggest bully and the most brutish of the brutes. Tough talk can no longer be a sign of leadership . . . collective consciousness is the future. Our prayer is that you are ready and willing -- because you're totally able . . . that you're not only willing -- you're inspired to resolve this fundamental human dilemma; that you listen to the feminine, whether inside yourself or inside others, and honor balance . . . not dominance.

There have been four ancient 'mastery-laden' civilizations -- ones that achieved phenomenal advancements in technology during previous tectonic eras. There's no "easily found" archaeological records of these moments on Earth -- except for that which will ultimately be discovered buried deep beneath the shifted continental plates. These four civilizations are referred to -- in metaphysics -- as 'Root Races' and we are now living in the 'Fifth Root Race'. The mythology is that each of these civilizations disappeared when their highly advanced technology outpaced the conscious awareness of their collective purpose. Whenever this happens, advanced technology loses 'compassion' as its essential partner. Without compassionate ideals as a partner to technology, technology defaults to being a partner with fear . . . it's then used for reasons without trust; without heartfelt connection, and ultimately without any healthy benefit. In the end, this cycle destroys its host . . . just like cancer does. Such were the fates of Atlantis and Lemuria -- two of the other four glaring examples of what happens when compassion and technology do not coexist. Compassion can be measured in many dimensions, but in none of these dimensions is the sensation of compassion all that exciting . . . it's very inspiring, but not very exciting. There's an entirely different motivation between these two emotions. Excitement actually comes from its play with uncertainty . . . the mysterious possibilities of something working, or not working out are powerful emotional stimulants. In the aftermath of this uncertain stimulation comes a great sense of personal entitlement. This phenomenon appears as a moment of conflicted interest – "what's in this for me," competes with, "how this best serves we." The answer in this moment holds either the seeds of greed, or the seeds of compassion. Our prayer is that you're a champion of the seeds of compassion; that you plant them within every effort, every project, and every moment you're connected to; that you give up your need for excitement, and allow the inspiration of compassionate moments to become the influence of your destiny on the fate of Mother Earth.

*F*rustration arrives to demonstrate the need for a change at the core level. Once this demonstration performs you must release frustration to enjoy the rest of the process . . . otherwise all change will be frustration. Our prayer is that you welcome frustration and then ride joy and inspiration through the changes.

Scientists from the University of Queensland, Australia, have used particles of light (photons), to show that light can pass through a wormhole -- a fold-over of spacetime -- and interact with an older version of itself. The source of this time-travel phenomena comes from what are called "closed timelike curves" (CTC) are extremely powerful gravitational fields . . . waves from a black hole. According to Einstein's theory of general relativity, these waves of gravity from CTC's can warp the fabric of existence so extremely, that spacetime actually bends back over itself like a Mobius-strip -- creating a pathway to travel backward or forward in time. This actually disrupts the laws of cause and effect (karma) -- and the wisdom keepers, of ancient civilizations, knew about this; they'd use these dimensional phenomena to clear events from their past. Everything that these ancient masters practiced in these advanced civilizations -- a history buried by the Earth's shifted tectonic plates -- are becoming measurable today by these new advancements in science. This clearing of past karma, masters referred to as "opening the mouth of time," is achieved by re-experiencing a moment, without any guilt from the moment. When you don't allow yourself to experience guilt, you remain wide-open to learn from the mistake. You can actually relive a previous moment, while it teaches you the better way of unfolding it. This takes tremendous discipline, to sit -- totally stable and unflinching, while the moment replays itself -- pain and all -- to demonstrate alternately available moments. At the end of this process, the best way forward is revealed; the complete lesson has been learned; the karma has served its purpose . . . it releases the emotional debris; the debt is deleted. Our prayer is that you use this innate ability to review your time with a mastery of life. Hold unfortunate moments, from the "past" of your existence; recapitulate them through your emotional stability -- forgive everyone (including yourself) -- absorb every lesson and return the moment to its natural joy. This is real . . . always has been real . . . it's even science now.

*D*ark matter and dark energy make up 95% of the universe . . . it's actually the raw material of future now. When you are committed to an outcome, this dark 95% contains what you require . . . it's like freeze-dried future . . . just add light and make it now. Our prayer is that you use your tools -- faith and trust -- prayer and meditation -- light up your commitment . . . create your future now.

Yoga and meditation practices developed in many parts of the world simultaneously. Relics in museums of pre-history, from Latin America, to Africa, to Asia display stone carvings and clay sculptures of yoga postures well over ten thousand years old. Then why did this only survive as a part of India's culture? From the east-west spin of the Earth -- and the resulting movement of the continental plates -- all major mountains ranges run north and south . . . except for the Himalayas. When the many Ice Ages descended on the Earth, the Himalayas protected the Indian subcontinent. In all the other parts of the world, the ice ages eliminated the normal human 'herbivore' food supply. The survivors resorted to eating anything that was left . . . an herbivore's diet became primarily carnivorous -- the gatherers became hunters. The results are found in the archaeological remains -- human ancestors, everywhere but South Asia, took on the territorial natures and habits of carnivores. Carnivores are the only animals that control territory . . . the 'glacial' lives of humans were reduced to the constant competition for their food and land. Violence was employed to control these lands, and the development of weapons turned the innovations of a benevolent mind -- into the martial nature of war, and a violent mind. In South Asia -- where the Ice Ages never touched -- the benevolent mind continued to develop the civility of yoga and meditation; nutritional vegetarian cuisine; ayurvedic herbal/mineral medicines and other naturally healthy practices; thread and weaving of the first fabric for clothing; sails were developed for boats and they explored further into the 'round' world; astronomy, astrology, higher math and science emerged. All of this was created from peaceful minds, and the sharing consciousness of benevolent communities. Our prayer is that you include meaningful moments of conscious self-discovery in your own daily routine; look closely to determine which habits are left-over subtle "violence" and which ones are benevolence . . . make gentle shifts . . . calm down your mind and world . . . "be the changes you want to experience."

*E*verything in this universe is in motion -- nothing can be stuck -- motion is the natural law of matter. When you are experiencing 'being stuck', you are experiencing a 'fantasmic' illusion of mind . . . not a reality at all. Our prayer is that you wake up from the fantasy, embrace the true reality, and move with your intentions knowing nature is on your side.

*E*motions are far more powerful than thoughts -- they can ignite; stimulate; discourage, or completely block life's energy in any moment. Boredom is perhaps the most misunderstood of all the emotion. Guru Nanak called boredom, "moderation" -- the Buddha referred to it as "the middle path." Boredom is the sensation that arrives without any extremes, when there's nearly always calm, and when all the other elements are in a state of natural balance. For those who require great stimulation, boredom is not a friendly place. However, boredom's greatest benefit is that it allows your full receptivity to take place. Because of the deep absence of activity, it allows for more contemplative and intuitive moments. In these moments, boredom nurtures a type of certainty; certainty brings a form of stability; stability can produce consistency, and consistency allows growth to take place any time, over time . . . the exact nature of nature. At the opposite end of nature, when growth takes place suddenly, it's nearly always corrected as an anomaly . . . unsustainable. This will then produce an instability; a fear and uncertainty -- which triggers excitement, counteracting boredom . . . causing an unconscious brain to embrace the pleasures of the distractions and disruptions. This gives the brain the sense that -- I need to solve a problem -- I better get busy . . . and there you have the main reason why the brain hates boredom . . . it does not appreciate inactivity. Alternatively, the more conscious person sits inside boredom; the focus drops from the problem-solving brain, to the connection-experiencing heart, and a deep meditation unfolds. Our prayer is that you're at ease whenever you are bored; that you take this opportunity to live in your meditative heart and give your brain a rest; dive deeply into this field of 'no-stimulation' and discover its easy, gently balanced atmosphere. Lose yourself in the ease of this balance and allow yourself to know and grow and rejuvenate.

Imagine for a moment, within the boundaries of your life, something outside the boundaries of your imagination. You're not imagining even close to your known 'self' . . . this image has never existed before . . . be willing to never exist again in this imagined form -- in this particular way. You're only existing in it within the imagined opportunities of this moment. Within this attitude, no others can completely embrace or appreciate you at first -- they'll criticize you, because they don't recognize you. You're still imagining, and within this image you're immune to the criticism -- not that you brush it off -- but you're actually, completely beyond it. An autoimmune system that's this strong indicates an extremely high self-value . . . it means your bio-logical system values this version of you so much, it's willing to protect it at all cost . . . you do not need sympathy. This self, that you're imagining, is actually the closest you can possibly fathom to who you actually are . . . who you (in some lifetime) will actually become. So, you've got to ask yourself the obvi-ous, "Why not now . . . when is now going to be the right time?" Realize something . . . this "now" can only exist if you lose your mind, if you release the preconceptions and allow the Universal mind to create your existence . . . the fullest extent of your existence. When you give yourself this gift -- this gift that you're imagining -- you've giving yourself your freedom . . . your birthright. This 'IS' your life -- fully experienced between the two extreme positions of pure gravitational logic, and pure levitation magic -- a life like the Buddha, Krishna and Jesus lived . . . a life of you being the highest you. Our prayer is that you give yourself the right to imagine this unimaginable opportunity; step into it as if it's meant to be; walk in these footsteps and experience the freedom as well as the fear . . . and when you fall down -- because it's so unfamiliar -- pick yourself back up; think nothing of the fall, and keep walking.

*A*s a master teacher -- one who allows each moment to speak for itself . . . bringing no pre-determination into it all -- the moments become a teacher to the master. Our prayer is that you are in love with your mastery and are always willing to learn something new.

The word confidence comes from 'confiance', which in French means 'faith'. When you're confident, you're not shielding your awareness, you're able to perceive all that surrounds you . . . even experiencing its polarities. The sensation of beauty can be found within an ugly moment . . . joy can be found within sorrow. Confidence makes it more likely to find these polarities. Neuroscience has begun to discover why. Studies show the brain's endogenous electrical field can transmit signals into the electromagnetic fields surrounding your body. These electromagnetic fields are what metaphysics calls your aura. Masters teach that when your aura is strong, you have more physical and mental awareness . . . and more confidence. Your brain transmits signals through your electromagnetic field; it travels out into your world and reflects back through this aura to your brain . . . it builds. If you think of beauty -- but the surroundings lack obvious beauty -- this thought reflects off your surroundings and the returning information inspires you, which transmits out and receives back more signals of beauty . . . this repeats over and over, self-reflecting millions of times every moment. It appears that beauty actually is in the eyes of the beholder. Also, when you're surrounded by people of faith, you'll experience more faith in their presence, as these new studies show -- in addition to your brain's signals traveling through your electromagnetic field, they also travel through the electromagnetic fields of the people around you. This is literally the makeup of a 'group aura'. Confidence is the emotional charge that turns this capacity on; allows this communication to happen; opens the brain to its power of transmission beyond the confines of your body. It uses both your aura, and the auras of others . . . the power of group consciousness. Our prayer is that you develop your confidence; open your aura to the beauty all around you; extend the power of your mind and leverage your faith to connect with others and achieve your goals through their presence . . . be the beholder of beauty . . . fill your eyes with it.

You are an event of life-charged within spacetime, assigned to face each moment as an equal within it, and to it. When you forget this specific detail of the assignment (which is the 'equals' part) your moments either overwhelm you or seem insignificant. In these ways your assignment turns into drama. Our prayer is that you adore the drama-free zone of your equality.

The history of the Universe has not always been heavy and grave. The history -- that's filled with wars -- is not so common in the larger picture. It's only the world you've come to know in the most recent times . . . the past hundred million years. Think of a world with far less gravity, and you're imagining a world that once existed . . . less gravity . . . more levity, and the possibilities this brings. You're viewing an ancient moment . . . when carpets could fly; when walking on water was a "walk in the park" . . . war was never used to settle anything, for with reduced gravity, everything's affected. In levity your thoughts have lightness; they're uplifting in every aspect -- full of light -- never heavy, or burdensome -- ideas are inspirational. This was common in ages past . . . the ruling ideas and consequential realities came out of thoughts with super-levity. Compared to today's world -- the one with barbaric violence that we consider reality -- this ancient world was 'Heaven on Earth'. What could've possibly been the science -- the explanation behind such a difference? The entire Universe is filled with the most abundant form of known matter in existence . . . this is plasma. Plasma is one of the four fundamental material states -- the others being solid, liquid and gas. Plasma has an exceptional amount of free electrons and ions . . . super-conductive . . . producing extraordinary electrical charges and electromagnetic fields. Storms of densely packed plasma winds are always passing through the Universe -- like weather patterns here on Earth. Astrophysics calls this the 'Electric Universe' with its massive 'mythological' thunderbolts traveling between planets, stars and galaxies. This makes for an entirely different and levitational field . . . a place where ideas are magical and objects are light like air; where imagination interacts at the level of the quanta to produce realities purely from your beliefs. Our prayer is that you prepare for this future -- the masters throughout time have been predicting its return – practice your lightness; lighten your thoughts; catch this new wave of your life, and ride it into the extraordinary realms of levity.

There is a dynamic silence to be found in the deeper regions of human consciousness; the dynamics of this silence are the teachers of teachers with lessons buried inside lessons that are inside lessons. The only way to visit these teachers is to give up living in the intellect's description of what is happening in life . . . a description is not an experience . . . you must allow your experiences to teach these lessons within lessons. Our prayer is that you give yourself time for dynamic silence each day to learn the lessons that live deep inside the inside of your experiences without thought.

Science studies enigmas – one enigma is the dinosaurs. Given what's known about their body size from all the remains -- with this 'mass to muscle' ratio -- there's no way they could have held up their heads, or even walked. The gravity, on Earth today, would have been too much for them to exist. In addition to the questions about the Earth's gravity at the time of the dinosaurs, it's widely acknowledged that their rapid demise was caused by a catastrophe. Somehow Earth's gravity and environment had changed, and changed abruptly . . . many times over. All this evidence confirms: a 'linear-logical' history of our planet, consistently unfolding over billions of years, is completely absurd. All science must open the doors to possibilities that explain these phenomenal discrepancies in the historical data. Think about some of the 'non-linear' possibilities that might explain -- not only this vastly decreased gravity, and the rapid demise of huge populations -- but the countless unexplained archeological findings. Imagine: there was a vastly different placement of the planets in our solar system, with life on many; a more highly charged electro-magnetic field, caused by plasma, surrounding the Earth and other planets; there's been many sudden shifts of the Earth's magnetic poles; life on other planets and solar systems have seeded life on Earth; highly enlightened populations of humans, lived millions of years ago at the magnetic poles. None of these are beyond the realm of possibilities when considering all the evidence that cannot currently be explained. There's an old saying: "The only difference between mythology and history is that mythology is true." When you think about some of the ancient myths and begin to piece together the physical evidence, you realize that history has not been linear, and it's definitely not been logical. Our prayer is that you question everything; create your own conclusions and test them against all that you've been led to believe; open your mind to the "unexplained" and allow the "explained" to be disproven . . . become a master of your own beliefs, and produce a mythology that supports your life within all life.

Wakefulness is available after all the struggles of existence have been surrendered. Since all struggle is self-orchestrated to imply great value in the effort, this surrender is very challenging to engage . . . it feels too much like giving up. Our prayer is that you know you are loved and allow this love to awaken you.

*B*utterflies, frogs and toads are those courageous creatures of incredible physical transformation. Each of them, at a moment in time, faced annihilation if they didn't take drastic measures. Their drastic measures produced a complete transformation in the way they lived. From a fish to a frog and toad . . . this journey takes place when the means of breathing water through gills is rapidly disappearing. The little innocent fish -- who has already sprouted legs and lost its tail -- thrusts it head out of the water in a desperate reach for air . . . its entire life changes forever as it ventures out onto three dimensional land. Caterpillars begin weaving their cocoons with unknown purpose, but the purpose is known to the knowing of nature. As the creature rests within the completion of this exhausting task, a battle suddenly erupts and destroys the peace within its body. Imaginal cells -- ones that have been with the caterpillar since birth -- begin to multiply rapidly and overwhelm the physical structure as it dissolves into chrysalis . . . a soupy gel of nothing in the moment. Out of these imaginal cells comes the imagination of a new greatness . . . a life of flight . . . the magnificence of a butterfly is born from this soupy chrysalis. These creatures are all barometers of the planetary health . . . the radiant body of Mother Earth is now reaching out . . . the same way as the body of the frogs and the caterpillars reached out for ways beyond the threshold of their own annihilation. These little creatures are all tuned to this calling of the Mother Earth . . . they've been there before, they recognize the landscape. They're currently advising that you're on that threshold; you're about to experience some dramatic evolutionary changes that aren't optional. Our prayer is that you're ready willing and able to be those barometers -- those seers who chart the maps -- the ones with imaginal cells that imagine a way forward in this moment of evolutionary crisis. And because you will not remain lost in the illusion of your own illusion, you'll be ready to merge with the radiant body of Mother Earth, and follow her instructions of nature that lead the way forward.

The next step is the step that is always available . . . this is a law of nature. Remembering this law whenever there's hesitation is a gift of presence, and presence is a gift of conscious breathing. Our prayer is that you consciously breathe and courageously take the next step and then the next and the next.

*P*erfectionism is a means that evolution has used for billions of years to get things right. As a matter of science, it's known -- evolution attempts up to fifty thousand ideas, to get one that works perfectly. It's perfectionism that finds that "one in the fifty thousand." Your world, by nature, is a world of these attempted perfections . . . the greater your awareness, the more you feel it's pull. Nearly everyone you know has the awareness of this evolutionary stimulant. Whenever you're on your path of awareness, you'll have an issue with perfection . . . it's just a part of the landscape. When you use perfection as a spice, it's a major achiever . . . as a diet, it's a progress blocker. Place definitions on perfection and those will be applied in many dimensions. One is the dimension of time . . . place limits on this fourth dimension and you'll stimulate progress. Another -- the three dimensions of space . . . place boundaries on space, and your efforts will more exactly define the outcome. All of these are examples of how this ancient evolutionary mechanism designs and defines your perfectly-imperfect world. Use these definitions wisely . . . apply the proper pressures to define, design, and reach your goals . . . perfection becomes your evolutionary friend. There are many characters inside you -- they all take part in this process -- each involved in your efforts. The more advanced you are, the more of these characters you can employ; the more you feel the effects of this perfectionism. But also, the more you feel plagued by the need to be perfect. Don't take this as a curse, realize its blessing . . . your advanced state is employing this blessing, with multiple characters, to expand the "limits" of time and space. Employ perfection as a positive -- it becomes your asset -- eventually you'll seem to have all the time and space in the world. Our prayer is that your sense of needing to be perfect is viewed -- not as a curse, but as an advanced sign of evolution -- that it becomes your friend, not you're enemy . . . and as a great buddy, it will assist you to define, design and achieve your imperfectly perfect goals.

Your "run" through your 'life-of-time' is best experienced as a marathon with radical stillness mixed in. This combination can only be believed and then understood in the world of reality that's also expanded into the world of make believe . . . the world in which you make up all of your own beliefs as if you have every right to do so. Our prayer is that you are skilled in the art of making the magical opportunities very believable.

Whenever you experience your animals, and you're left with that sense of compassion . . . you're experiencing their natural connection beyond time. This compassionate connection serves all life, a connection of unison that makes your animals so special, and such great teachers. You experience this as their master, but stop and entertain a moment when you're the creature; they're the "master." You've seen a large flock of birds . . . a school of fish . . . all moving in unison without the slightest visible sign of what causes the instant shift in direction. This is that connection beyond time; it works amongst a species, and across species. It connects you and your animals; you and your loved ones; you and your co-workers. Animals have this naturally wired into their 'non-choices' . . . you can activate this in your relations. It turns on a higher level of communication that's effortless, compassionate and simultaneous. Such is the nature of a 'cultural' vision and/or mission . . . just like the flock of birds it creates unison and harmony. Think of your relations between family and co-workers as the quantum possibilities of an undisturbed particle – like dice flying through the air -- a blur of spinning opportunities, not yet noticed; not yet observed, assigned, or chosen. Within this state of possibilities (the dice still in the air), there's a moment of choice . . . the dice hit the table as one of the possibilities. For you, this landing is your choices; your entire system is wired for choices . . . you make them several times each moment . . . they range from a complete mess, to total success. Because your animals do not have these choices, their vision and mission are their connections . . .

moving in unison . . . living in peace . . . being productive . . . achieving success . . . all the 'relational missions' of nature. Our prayer is that you set your relations to capture the highest possibilities of connection within each moment; follow the lead of your animals and emulate their 'non-choice' behavior with your choice of a 'vision and mission' that cause the 'random' nature of nature to become the opportunities for your greatest success.

*O*pening the mouth of time is like opening the mouth of an alligator -- once opened and staring you directly in the face, there are countless sensations all driven by the same option . . . the total desire to survive the ordeal. The mouth of time, like the alligator, will eventually get to you as you learn . . . it's all about the "journey" through the moments. Our prayer is that your "journey" through the moments is as complete and fulfilling as you can possibly imagine . . . with every breath dedicated to every breath.

Just as the eyes and ears receive optical and auditory information and relay it to the brain -- your heart is the sensory relay that receives the information of love from the ocean that envelops all life; then relays this to the brain. Living with an "open heart" receives the most of this information -- just as living with your eyes and ears open allows you to see and hear the most of what's around you. However, an open heart, in a dangerous setting, by nature feels unsafe. But, if you hold it open long enough, this produces greater awareness, one that perceives beyond the danger. Your natural reaction to shut down is actually the more dangerous reaction . . . it closes off this perception. Being open around danger delivers intuition . . . gives you the insight to solutions. For every challenge, or danger, there's an equal solution in the immediate vicinity . . . this is nature's law. The world today is no more dangerous than the world of a million years ago -- it's just that a million years ago you worried about a sabretooth tiger; today you have to deal with the sabretooth neighbor. The idea that you can be safest when you're experiencing love is counter-intellectual, and counter-emotional . . . everything about danger tells you to shut down, run and hide. However, when you ride your thoughts and emotions -- in the midst of this danger -- it's like riding a wild horse; you're actually safest when not fighting the animal, but when you're intuitively anticipating the animal's presence and movements. In this way you're tuning to your awareness more than your emotions; this awareness of the "horse" allows for a successful ride, not just achieve safety. Our prayer is, when you're caught in a challenging scene; you're in the vicinity of that sabretooth "tiger" of your life -- in combination with every-thing else that you're doing -- ride the emotions and thoughts; anticipate their movements and feel them registering at the cen-ter of your pounding chest . . . right there in the heart. You'll discover the answers and the solutions with your openness to an overwhelming sense of self-love . . . your open heart is the safest place you can live.

When the quantum mechanics of the Spirit dimensions meet the material mechanics of spacetime, there is an event that science calls chaos. This is the realm of the miraculous and is a perfect location to work with the theta-states of your meditative brain. Our prayer is that you meditate here daily and expect miracles to follow you.

*A*ngels and guides ride amongst the waves in the ocean of love . . . a calm courage in a space that's always chaotic. Quantum Physics says this chaos initiates material reality, but it doesn't, it's actually the raw material of reality. The initiator is your bold imagination . . . both conscious and unconscious . . . loving and critical. When life's fortune leads you to some-one with whom you experience this calm courage within the chaos -- even if it's only for a brief moment -- this is an angel in your life . . . a divine guide. This pure experience -- this sacred partner -- will encourage your boldest imagination and inspire the strength you require to believe in it. This is vital nourish-ment to your extraordinary life -- whether for a moment, or forever -- this person is a devotee of your soul. Your task in such a relation -- even when the window is brief -- is to honor this 'vein' of devotion. Like a vein of precious metal inside the Earth of mundane stones -- follow it as it guides you to the source . . . the source of all life's sacred journeys. This angel will guide you with encouragement and bring calm to the chaos of many lifetimes. This angel may be your love -- your life partner -- an animal in your world -- or an occasional friend or stranger pushing you toward your fulfillment . . . be deeply grateful for them all, for gratitude is the food of their angelic experience . . . and you have many angels. Whenever their guidance fades or disappears . . . sit within the surrounding chaos -- embrace their memory and their calming sensations . . . this vein of consistency you once sensed, will eventually reappear and carry you safely forward. Our prayer is for your gratitude in the times of guidance and the times of waiting for it to reappear; for mastering your bold imagination and igniting a sacred reality within the chaos of these times. Calling all angels . . . respond well to their calm encouragement as you play in life's storms.

*U*nreasonable knowing is a leveraging belief that you can apply to time in order to stretch, shrink, bend and shape it. Having leveraging beliefs is essential for maintaining human freedom. Our prayer is that your love for freedom is so great that you honor your unreasonable knowing and spend time each day learning to master it.

*P*eople are always curious, how to know if what they're sensing is intuition, or just an emotional charge. The answer is usually quite simple, intuition leaves no emotional trail; does not arrive with even the slightest emotional attachment . . . not even a tiny one. Intuition is an excellence of your total awareness; arrives without preference or attachment to the revelations involved, and then leaves you neutral . . . with options. It's a bit of a magician that way. Whenever there's a preference or attachment to an outcome, the sensation you're experiencing is the charge surrounding an emotional focal point. This is not intuition, but the result of an emotion penetrating the question. Intuition is incredibly calm -- yet it permeates everything around it with its revelations . . . there's a big difference between this permeating nature and how an emotion penetrates. Humans nuance their emotions, often without accurately or completely expressing them. The accurate unexpressed emotions are then invisibly stored inside your emotional body, waiting for another opportunity to express their preferences . . . often blurting into awkward moments with impassioned certainty -- posing, of course, as intuition. This is not intuition -- it's a very convincing emotional charge. You can unconsciously live within these multiple layers of incomplete emotional expression -- holding their disruptive patterns layered within other unexpressed preferences . . . all the while maintaining deep attachments . . . waiting to awaken and pose as intuition. Our prayer is that you practice being bold enough to make your move; permeate your inner world with the awareness of these layers -- admitting that you have them is a good place to start. Express them into your meditations; then -- when they've been expressed -- gently practice using intuition to guide you forward. Living intuitively will eventually become your very rewarding reward.

What science measures as the age of the universe is just the distance within a single trough of spacetime . . . like a wave on the ocean, this wrinkle in the fabric of spacetime is hardly the entire ocean. Yet it is all we can perceive of our universe from within the depth of the trough we are in. The actual mass and age of our universe is so much larger than this that it's comical when compared. Our prayer is that you understand this universe is not billions, but quadrillions of years old and then love, honor and cherish your life in the grandness and freedom of this scale.

There's no being in love and being out of love -- not the way it's used in current conversations -- that's just a fantasy expression. Love is a universal constant – abundantly, everywhere always. You're always in love; you reside in an ocean of it. Saying unconditional love is like saying 'love—love' . . . love is always unconditional . . . you are either experiencing it, or you aren't. To experience this love requires the openness in your heart to be aware of this universal constant. This takes courage -- which means 'a time of the heart' -- because love leaves you highly vulnerable. The willingness to remain vulnerable, in this current world of 'great perceived danger', would be considered extremely foolish to the perspective of "logic." That's why it has been said throughout history that "fools rush in." However, having the sense of love is in fact an actual sense; it's as obvious as having any other sense. There's a pathway through the heart, just as there's an auditory, and an optical pathway for those senses. To have the sense of love you must allow this pathway, through the heart, to remain open in the face of all the input . . . even danger. Humans also once had a botanical sense – one that could tell us, just by approaching a plant – whether it was medicine, food, or poison. You've lost this sense, because when you began to cultivate your food you no longer used it . . . what you don't use, you will lose. Humans have lost a great deal of the ability to sense the ocean of love, because when you live in constant fear -- whether a high, or low level fear -- you don't want love to obscure the messages of danger. To remain in your heart in the midst of these messages -- to remain aware of the ocean of love you are in -- requires great courage, great strength and a great sense of self-confidence. Our prayer is that you reestablish all of your lost senses; truly become a self-sensory human and master of your environment. Welcome the messages that these sense have to deliver, and bath in their miracles in the ocean of love . . . miracles surrounded by danger, that's the nature of love . . . safety in the midst of peril . . . be the fool and love it.

*O*ur Universe is a bubble amongst many bubbles arising from the infinite void . . . to believe that there is only one Universe is to discount the enormity of infinity. These bubbles that make up the fabric of spacetime are In fact the multi-verse. Our prayer is that you transform your thinking to accommodate the true magnitude of your incredible existence.

*M*edical science has discovered that ninety percent of the brain's energy is being used in ways that are unknown; totally unaccounted for. Where does this energy go? What's it doing? None of these questions have yet been answered by science. Considering that your brain uses twenty percent of your body's total energy output, this medical mystery represents eighteen percent of your actual life-energy . . . that's a lot. Science knows that the brain is always looping signals through a series of pathways -- neurons and brain tissue. These are the signals of your life as you move through your moments. The brain traces and then retraces these steps . . . over and over with great obsession, like a map maker would. The scenes on these maps are the three known brain functions: sensory (what's happening); behavioral (what can I do), and limbic (what does it mean). But then science loses track of the "map" as ninety percent of the energy vanishes into the shadows and wanders beyond the limits of three dimensional space and the fourth dimension of time . . . out into pure "wilderness." Here it uses this ninety percent of its total energy -- seemingly doing "nothing" -- the "nothing" that's a great mystery to neuroscience. Ancient pictographs of diverse cultures depicted a fascination with this mystery. Then, hundreds of thousands of years later -- yogis, great seers, and spiritual masters began charting and mapping this unknown world with their enlightened meditations. They're answers were: this energy maintains your connection to the soul, and all of its relationships in the cosmos. This is a channel that's always open for communication, but one that few people are ever aware of. This is a map of the dimensions that are waiting in the human future, waiting for you to awaken. Once this awakening takes place, it will be as revolutionary as the first use of fire; the discovery of the wheel, and the "flat-Earth" becoming round. Our prayer is that you awaken to this journey; that you're one of the pioneers that alters the course of human history; that you relate to these maps as a real responsibility, not a future fantasy . . . and you welcome this mission as if it's right now.

The cycles of spacetime move far, far beyond any ability to imagine them, and our lives can ride these limitless waves far beyond 100 years; yet our life expectancy hangs on thin threads within an imagined fabric of old-age limitations. The common way of addressing these limits is with childish commotion and crisis, but the best way to break the old and master a new habit is with consistent good food, yoga and deep meditations. Our prayer is that you choose these restful ways to remake your expectations by creating a -- long-life -- life-long -- set of these daily healthy habits.

Consciousness sits within the observed four dimensions of our collective human agreement and is trapped by this until it's released by the authority of our higher awareness. This authority comes from within and is governed by the balance or imbalance of belief. Our prayer is that you believe you have this authority to be the authority in your life, and give yourself the power to observe a great day . . . each and every day.

When you want to connect; when you want to create a relationship, the most vital action to take is to deeply listen. All relationships and connections are circles . . . enclosed combinations of projections and receptions. Amongst humans, and any creature with verbal communication, reception is listening -- projection is expressing. Sunia is the word in Sanskrit/Gurumukhi that means: the art of 'extreme deep listening' . . . beyond the words . . . listening to the tones; to the inflections; to the inferences -- each subtlety of the sound. It's through these subtleties that you actually connect to the root understanding -- what a person truly means; where they've come from to speak their words; what they're intending with these words, and how sincere . . . absolutely everything. Even when they're unable to accurately express the exact words, these subtleties express the missing information for them . . . such is the art of sunia . . . deep listening. When a person experiences your depth of listening -- their needs will relax . . . they feel heard. Once a person feels heard, they're able to further express their feelings and thoughts; their communication becomes more authentic; a deep relation and connection takes place. In today's world, this is an avoided art . . . listening at this deepest level feels too vulnerable . . . it exposes too much information. Instead, it's become a common human reaction to not listen to someone's words, but to interpret instead . . . to determine what their words mean to the listener -- not the speaker. Our prayer is that you will stop interpreting and start listening; be willing to receive a connection within a conversation; listen to the layers of another person's expression; understand the purpose behind their words, as well as the missing words too timid to be spoken. Practice 'sunia' and create an authentic connection with each conversation. Enable understanding by standing under the communication of each relationship and lifting it up . . . or as Yogi Bhajan would say, "In every conversation, be a forklift."

*B*reathing is about receiving the gift of yet another moment, never about holding the memory of the ones gone past. When you disengage the thoughts of past and future and focus on the gift of this moment of life, you are able to truly appreciate breathing. Our prayer is that you are grateful for what is and carry it to the depth of each breath.

*G*ravity has been around since the beginning of matter. When no one understood what gravity was, and how it worked, the world was "flat." But even when the world was "flat," the world was round . . . that's the omnipresence of gravity. Wind has also been around since the beginning of matter, yet it took billions of years for life to discover how to use the wind . . . spinning thread; weaving the thread into cloth; sewing sails; setting up the sail with an equal keel. Each of these steps took hundreds of thousands, even millions of years to master through trial and error. Gravity will be the wind of the future, for just like wind, it's a directional force. One advantage to gravity, over wind, is that the direction and presence of gravity is constant. Beyond the Earth, gravitational waves have also been discovered rolling between planets, even between star-systems . . . this will provide a new window into the entire universe. We will sail on it around the Earth; use it as a constant source of energy; travel space and even deep space . . . a real star trekker with warp speeds. The even greater advantage of this system of propulsion is that, like the wind, no one owns its source. When no one owns the source of an omnipresent energy, there is no territory to dispute over ownership. The fundamental nature of the human is herbivorous; herbivores are all 'non-territorial' animals . . . the human has no 'gene' to instinctually know how to successfully own "territory" . . . therefore humans resort to endless wars over it . . . which is the most senseless nature of the [not] human nature. This energy is the future that will bring peace . . . giving humans the time, without war, to solve their dilemmas and move on to the task of universal enlightenment. Our prayer is that you look at the parts of your world that are territorial; discover ways in which you can release this 'awkward' version of your vision; welcome others into your space and your time, whether virtual or actual, and allow for your real nature to become your human nature. This will bring the peace that's essential for life to survive . . . the entirety of life on the planet Earth will rejoice when war is over.

*P*urusha is the endless, unchanging, uncaused, present everywhere, connecting everything and yet completely invisible nothing . . . the nothing that produces everything . . . the infinite void. Our prayer is that you honor the enormity of this vastness without trying to fully understand it because you can't. Rest in the comfort of knowing that you know without any proof of knowing.

*H*ere's your world -- a gift of life from 'Infinity'. 'Infinity' is the giver with the ability to deliver anything and produce everything. One of the best parts of this world of gifts is when you're ready and able to receive them . . . and then, working on your 'willingness to receive' is the assignment of a lifetime. To open this 'willingness to receive' -- Infinity has employed legions of angels (a legion is 4,444) -- all guiding and guarding you through each phase of the lesson. Some of these angels are the people around you, such as relatives and friends, and then there are the angelic strangers . . . people you don't even know -- or perhaps never know. One of the greatest sources of angelic assistance are your pets and animals -- these angels have come into this world to be closer to you than any person could ever be. One of the pre-requisites of an angel is the unending ability of forgiveness -- dogs, cats, horses and other animals have this quality mastered . . . and when they don't use it . . . there's a very good reason. All animals have several bodies beyond their physical -- one of which is the multi-faceted emotional body. Each emotion is either used as a tool in life, or you unconsciously stumble under its influence. Studies have now shown that domesticated animals can mimic human emotional expressions in a split-second just like people . . . this shows empathy. These same researchers are going to eventually discover that all domesticated animals -- and even animals in the wild -- have the same emotional abilities as humans . . . simply a vastly different language through which they're expressed. Great seers have long been aware that these so called "pets" -- animals who've become very close to their masters -- are actually fully enlightened souls that have returned to life on Earth as angelic guides and guards to teach their masters that lesson -- the 'willingness to receive'. Our prayer is that you relate to your animals, knowing that they are your angels; gratefully accept their devotion, and more 'willingly receive' their blessings. As you sense the devotion . . . acknowledge it . . . as your teacher, they'll be so very grateful.

*A*s spiritual beings we perform our daily practice before the rise of the sun in order to navigate the waves of spacetime before they're stirred up with thoughts, feelings and actions. This is the time that's called 'amrit vela' which means veil of nectar. Our prayer is that you give yourself the opportunity to experience this sweet nectar on a daily basis.

*E*very moment is experienced in the microcosm of your breathing. Every breath is completely new; every moment is completely reborn within the breath. Inspiration means 'in-spirit' -- it's rebirthing into the new and unfamiliar. If you require safety, if you need it to be obvious in the foreground, then you will bring old memory into the moment and not experience the newness. You'll experience desperation -- which means 'without spirit' without rebirthing. You have a choice at the moment with each inhale . . . inspiration or desperation, or some combination of the two, and life becomes the accumulation of these choices. Life has a natural sense of security stored in the background, but when you require safety in the foreground, you bring in desperation . . . old familiarities obscure this natural security and no matter how much safety is provided, you'll always experience fear. Evolution, for survival reasons, has caused life to become the combination of 'this fear, and its need for safety'. This common modern lifestyle is referred to as: "being on top of things," but it's without inspiration -- eventually it's only desperate. It's choices that you've made . . . these choices accumulate . . . they're contained within the life-view that you experience and express. Every exhale contains the expressions of these choices -- the ones you've been making on your inhales. This forms the microcosm of your life -- inhales and exhales -- experiences and expressions . . . on and on . . . a breath leading to another breath. All of this is stored in the subconscious and ultimately becomes automatic. This is why your experience and your expressions are so vital. Our prayer is that you clear your subconscious, just like you take a shower in the morning; make life new with unfamiliarity and inspiration -- add positive memories -- experience the adventure and enjoy the natural security . . . now you'll "be on top of the world."

The universal creative principle that is prakriti is the 'something' that arises from nothingness . . . from the void known as Purusha. It changes, evolves and creates itself anew, time after time -- life after life, and is subject to the laws of cause and effect -- action and reaction. Our prayer is that you make the most of your relationship to this vast creative power and produce the day that you dream of every day.

The 'Hubble Space Telescope' has recently picked up stunning images of two galaxies merging and forming a new giant elliptical mega-galaxy. It seems -- when examining data from ancient micro-wave signals -- these merging mega-galaxies are occurring far more often now than at any time over the billions of years in the history of this universe. As a result of their motions, galaxies and smaller galaxies -- affected by each other's massive gravitational pull -- are gradually merging and combining . . . building ever larger structures. As the galaxies "collide" -- it's important to note -- the stars don't crash into each other, but synchronize their individual motions into a new collective motion. This is the same nature of sub-atomic particles (quantum); the nature of atoms; the nature of molecules; the nature of planets, the nature of the galactic nature; the nature of the universal structure -- these patterns are repeated at every level from the tiniest quanta to the most massive galactic scales, all working and sharing with each other at the highest levels of harmony. The only process that fights this pattern that's everywhere, is human nature . . . humans are the disruptive, destructive outlier. Imagine: galaxies merging together, collaborating, and cohabitating mutual space without destruction. When it's happening properly in the macrocosm -- what then can is so disrupting the human-cosm? If stars don't destroy each other with their mergers -- human differences can certainly coexist . . . the differences are able to be combined without fatal collisions. In order for humans to align, to live up to their assumed position as the highest life form on the planet, they'll need to synchronize with everything that surrounds and supports life. Our prayer you break from typical human nature; commit to participate in the more harmonic play; live in alignment with all things; learn from the quantum and from the universe, and teach by example to those you have differences with. Live in unity amongst all the diversity . . . without collisions.

The base coat of all colored paint is the neutrality of white; the base coat of all sound is silence; the base coat of all time is now; the base coat of all thought is a silent mind and its opportunity for ultimate creativity to mold the moment into momentum. The base coat of all emotions is joy; the base coat of all life is the soul; the base coat of all confusion is intuition and knowing. Meditations, when done consistently, take you to the base coat of consciousness which is total peace within total motivation. Our prayer is that you ride the sails of your moments to the base coat of every circumstance.

Spacetime -- commonly referred to as 'reality' -- is perceived remarkably different by different observers. With all their different 'velocities' . . . those unique perceptions produce opinions, conclusions, decisions, and ultimately the supporting thoughts and feelings. It's a fact of science -- every person has their own unique 'velocity' like a virtual fingerprint. These 'velocities' are both external and internal . . . three-dimensional, and virtual. The internal velocity is sensory perception experienced through the movement of your brain-mind connection, measured in 'frames' or 'cycles' per second. The external velocity is your physical movement through three-dimensional space. The combination of these two velocities produces the fourth dimension of time . . . both the logic of this time, and the non-logical sensations of time. The discrepancy, the difference, or comparison between these two forms of time -- leads to a majority of the problems/challenges amongst the observers . . . the people. Since these observations with all the opinions, conclusions, decisions, thoughts and feelings -- produce the phenomena of the experience . . . to think of it as a 'reality' is actually a 'fantasy'. Masters would call this fantasy . . . the illusion . . . the maya. Now, think of this more boldly, more proactively: if you give yourself the authority to be your unique velocity; to observe all phenomena, in your experience, through your own unique velocity -- then you give yourself the right to be you . . . with your vision, mission, and purpose, your total uniqueness . . . to really be you. Our prayer is that you make your move to be this bold; commit to a daily process that convinces you of who you truly are in practical terms; launch this as a commitment so that it obligates you to be proactive when you'd rather hide; rejuvenate yourself . . . be bold and don't ever fold.

*F*our-legged creatures live without the fourth dimension of time, they simply live in space. This is why they are so in the moment and important. The human creature must now graduate from this fourth dimension of time, into the dimension beyond time, and back into the infinite moment of the fifth dimension. Yet, there is no way of knowing a new dimension until you enter and experience it. Therefore, since entering the dimension beyond time is unknown, and what keeps us from this dimension is our fear of the unknown . . . our prayer is that you embrace the new to be renewed every day in the eternal moment.

In the human body you've been given many subtle components that -- if you learn how to use them -- can connect you to your greatest resources. This is the next evolution . . . mastering this human equipment and mastering life, but the world avoids this phase with over consumption and war. Everything that's been designed outside the self, mimics some part of this equipment that's inside. Even the wheel is just the blood cells rolling single file through the capillaries. Telephony is just externalizing telepathy. Quantum computing, long a challenge in the eyes of technology -- owing to microchip conflicts between electronics and photonics, is right there inside your brain . . . no conflict at all. However, the human brain uses less than 2% of its processing capacity -- and that's on a good day -- the rest is either locked in the subconscious mind, or the higher conscious mind. Yogis and masters, for thousands of years, have described all the universal wisdom that has come through their epigenetic inheritance. They teach that for seven generations, the DNA and RNA influence your physical, emotional, and mental worlds. "Impossible" is how modern biologists once reacted to this claim of inheritance. In recent years, however, researchers have found examples that prove the masters are correct . . . their teachings to be true. Yogis and masters use far more than this 2% limit of the brain, and that's how they access this unknown knowledge. The very same bandwidth and power density problems that create performance bottlenecks in microchips are found in the unenlightened mind. Expanding your belief; expands your mental performance -- then, when your belief expands to a tipping point -- you begin using light in place of electro-chemistry -- that's why it's called enlightenment. Use this light, and you're quantum computing . . . you're masterful . . . the universal wisdom is fully exposed. Our prayer is that you take full advantage of your human advantage; see the light in the darkness, and believe your way into this quantum world . . . here, you will solve the unsolvable; reform the deformed, and deliver a brighter future . . . being the light.

Sound is a vibration that occurs within the audible range of human hearing. Mantras are a collection of consonants and vowels as syllables that maximize this sound for the human body, mind and Spirit to respond to. Chanting mantra is like gargling with sound right down through the throat to the diaphragm. Our prayer is that you love to chant mantras.

*T*he fundamental desire of all life is to be absolutely connected with all life . . . anything less than this connection will be experienced as some form of pain -- physical, emotional, mental, or existential pain. Life seeks to avoid such pain in any way it can. Connecting to avoid the pain of separation is the basis of romance . . . connecting and correcting the pain of separation. The ultimate connection -- the ultimate romance -- is romancing the soul . . . connecting to that which connects everything. With this connection there's no separation anywhere in your life, anywhere in the world . . . anywhere in the universe. You experience absolute union -- the meaning of the word 'yoga'. One of the ways this 'yoga' has been practiced over the millennia is to connect with the magnificence in everything. Known as Raj Yoga (royal union), it uses rhythms and mantras -- aloud or silent -- combined into what's called 'Naad' . . . a constant mantra in the mind. It delivers a sensation of vastness -- of 'headroom' to each moment -- the sensation of being completely free. With this freedom there are no blockages; you have the probability of every possibility; ideas and solutions for each moment are inside of each moment . . . you're virtually "unstoppable." Of course, with this incredible freedom, you must now deal with the 'equal and opposite' -- it's the law of nature. The equal and opposite of total freedom is the daunting sensation that you have no right, you have no authority to be so free. This is life's natural reaction; the only way around this is for you to be 'self-authorized' -- give yourself the authority -- no one can do this for you. It's called Raj Yoga for a reason -- the universal authority of royalty. Our prayer is that you connect with your life each day; give yourself the authority to have massively creative freedom; use this freedom to design the world you want to live in, and live in this world with everyone you know . . . with love, with joy and inspiration, be benevolently royal.

When enthusiasm overrides common sense, it's time to pause and allow the wave of time to catch up with your effort. You just took an enthusiastic dip into the future and the present needs time to arrive. Our prayer is that you take these times to pause within your enthusiasm and allow effort to become effortless.

Imagine . . . you're going away on vacation, packing and prepping for your adventure, and you notice your dog looking very upset. You're planning on taking the dog, you've said this many times, but your dog doesn't know this for sure, it doesn't have the awareness to understand your assurances. He/she sits amongst your luggage with that worried look of being excluded. These doubts make this experience, in your pet's world, deeply troubling and eliminate any joy from their moment. When it could be enjoying the anticipation of being included, it troubles away the time. How much greater is your belief system . . . does your life also trouble away some of the moments like this? The universe is always packing for the adventure of your dreams -- that's the law of dreaming -- you cannot dream anything that cannot be achieved . . . everything you dream is available to you. When you doubt that you'll be included in, or allowed to experience your next destination -- you have no joy to enjoy it with. How different are you from the dog when you doubt the universe will include you on the journey of your dreams? There's little difference, for when you're limited by disruptive emotions, you're no longer able to sense the universal assuredness that you're loved . . . that's the 'universal law of love'. Just as your pet is loved by you and everyone around you, the universe loves and cherishes you in that very same way. You can fulfill all your dreams when you let the love take place . . . you are included. Our prayer is that you understand the laws of dreaming -- whatever you're dreaming, you're capable of achieving . . . it's here, it is waiting for you . . . it's the law. Release the doubt that's disrupting your faith; accept universal love beyond your wildest imagination; include yourself in fulfilling the most imaginative time of your life, and allow for the space to receive it. This is the law . . . please obey it.

*E*very day we must access the mechanisms of our lives and determine what is running our world. Is it our inner vision, or is it the outer circumstances? Then it's important to calculate to what degree each is involved. Inner vision promotes your destiny and outer circumstance is in league with your limits. Our prayer is that your inner vision, your destiny, is far more than fifty percent, and is the default leader of your life at all times.

*L*ight is found in two forms . . . waves and particles. Waves are what we see and particles (photons) are invisible, but we can use them. There are photons of light throughout the cosmos wherever there's a light-source, such as the sun at the center of our own star-system. When you tune in to your higher consciousness, your brain creates a direct connection with these photons through what spiritual masters refer to as your crown center. The crown center is governed by the pineal gland which gives you your sense of time, and time being enough . . . this is very calming. When activated, the pineal gland is nurtured and stimulated by light photons -- it literally feeds on light. You activate the pineal through deep meditation, dreaming and consciously focusing on and tuning into your highest thoughts. This can be done in many ways . . . collectively . . . personally . . . you can do it outwardly, or silently, with little notice, or with great enthusiasm. It's what's commonly referred to as devotion, and so often it's assumed that devotion is a very calm and inward process . . . but great exuberance and enthusiasm can be devotion too. Because the pineal regulates your relationship with time, when you tune in and turn on this gland often enough . . . you become enough . . . and when you experience the sensation of being enough, you feel you've got all the time in the world . . . forever becomes just a moment. This is very liberating. At such a moment you sense that you're equal to anything you face . . . within this sense you are super-open to solutions. Situations that appeared like monsters, become your equals -- become your partners . . . when your monsters become your partners, they're your friends . . . you have no more monsters. Our prayer is that you tune in to your higher self each day; turn on the pineal gland and use the sunlight (even in the clouds) to lighten your life . . . to shift your sense of time. When you do this, your monsters/problems become your friends, and solutions that seemed so far away, become just a moment away . . . then right here, right now.

In all that we face from moment to moment, whenever we are offended we have subscribed to the offense and adopted it into our sense of self. The only defense to this offense is deep neutrality, instant forgiveness, and a kind curious sense of humor. Our prayer is that whenever you are offended, you cancel your subscription, forgive yourself, and let out a sweet chuckle to release it.

As science looked through time -- geology took the story of this Earth, back beyond where archaeology and anthropology began . . . tracking the clues into remote corners of antiquity. But even then, the story of life -- and of human life -- is just an estimate from the logic in these clues. Three distinct journeys -- geology looks at Earth's patterns; archeology and anthropology look at life patterns . . . we've learned lessons from each, but they lack the subtle associations and magical connections . . . essentials that transform the clues into a photograph of time. These subtler components are found in the existential studies . . . the ones that approach antiquity from angles, nuances and inclinations. Philology, etymology and linguistics -- particularly with the languages of sacred mantra, prayer and humanology . . . these track the weave of language associations into the earliest moments of advancing life. They study life as it's becoming human -- becoming sacred -- and the complex journey it took . . . a journey of mystical texts and mantric languages. The word language means to 'gauge the 'lang' . . . the 'depth'. There are many vital explanations and crisscrossed associations found in sacred scriptures and mantras . . . subtle clues to a true history . . . defining precise pathways of enlightened living. These studies have shown that times of spiritual evolution run parallel to the expansion of the arts, music, science, math and language. They describe a road to enlightenment that's self-initiated and explored with great courage . . . one that projects this self-initiation from dimensions beyond hard logic. We're right in the middle of such a magical time once again; your life has every opportunity to take full advantage, of this advantage . . . to open your conscious, creative channels wide . . . without limits. Our prayer is that you do this; that you comprehend the magnitude of this moment where you live . . . the historical significance of the time. This is the 'age of enlightenment' all over again, and the language within your mind is ready to map your pathway forward . . . go ahead . . . have faith and take the steps . . . they're yours to take.

*I*llusion is the course of all existence . . . the nature of the fabric of spacetime. Authenticity is the opportunity within the weave of the fabric, setting up the pattern that travels through it all. Our prayer is that you exist authentically within the illusion of the fabric of your spacetime.

The beauty of suffering -- told by every great master -- is that it gives you a gauge, a compass on the dashboard of your life, to guide you toward joy, toward ease, knowing and liberation . . . liberation from greater suffering. When you're life is heading off course -- and you begin to suffer -- if you don't correct your course, but stubbornly maintain that off-course, direction . . . then you'll suffer even more. The more you complain about it, the more you'll suffer, because you're not listening. But if you use this suffering as a gauge, as a guide to direct you back on course -- toward your benevolent destiny -- then the suffering ends . . . you operate in alignment with that destiny. Just as when your hand comes near a hot stove, the hand experiences the heat; if you didn't feel anything, but placed your hand on the stove, you'd burn. Suffering is that warning, that sensation -- it's the way the physical world tells you; the emotional world tells you; the mental world tells you . . . hey, you're about to make a mistake -- about to walk down the wrong path . . . change now. We don't control what happens in life, we can control how we respond to it. When handled respectfully, suffering becomes a gentle, sacred guidance system in a life that makes good sense . . . and grows. There's one challenge -- when you think of it as punishment, or as a condemnation that you're bad -- then suffering becomes magnified . . . becomes a roadblock to your growth. Our prayer is that you embrace your suffering as a guide; open to the directives that it sends you; follow these directives and then live without suffering. Always be grateful -- grateful that it's right there -- benevolently waiting to guide you back on course . . . it's a friend.

The first chakra governs our physical survival; the second chakra our external approval and the third chakra tends to our internal approval . . . our nourishing of self through digestion. It's clearly time to better understand the universal balance existing throughout this region of our body by deeply studying and appreciating its support of life. Our prayer is that you practice this science of appreciation, within the art of compassion . . . every day . . . immediately upon awakening.

*E*nthusiasm and inspiration are free for the taking -- all that is required is being so inclined. Doubt -- on the other hand -- is very costly, it can cost you your dreams, and far more. The pathway to enthusiasm and inspiration passes through hope and courage, and once you arrive, it's self-sustaining . . . once you get them started, they reinforce each other like a great belly laugh. When you find yourself caught in the middle of this self-sustained sensation, you may find the faint questioning as to your right and your authority. This is when your right and your authority must have no reason, other than hope and courage, for this then becomes unreasonable and has no ability to be questioned. You will just be told that you are being unreasonable, to which you can answer, "Yes!" with great enthusiasm. This is why the best form of inspiration and enthusiasm -- is unreasonable -- it cannot be broken down with doubt -- and it re-delivers hope and courage -- steps up and defends itself unreasonably . . . right there, without hesitation. With each time you're confronted, you will be gifted with a free dose of courage, for they are all centered in the heart -- the cour -- and they fully support each other. This is freedom. As you become more inclined to act in this manner, you'll discover this self-sustaining energy creates great effort without effort . . . now you are operating with leverage -- the leverage of inspiration and enthusiasm. Our prayer is that you accept your right and your authority to be as inspired and enthusiastic as you like, any time you like; when questioned, give a huge smile; when laughed at, laugh along. Your health and your wealth will be grateful.

Tension pressure stress and friction are a part of all physical matter. As seen in a drop of water it holds matter together. Without these four qualities our lives could not exist. Our prayer is that you use these tools before they use you and find this to be useful in the fullness of your life.

*Y*our courage demonstrates self-value. Your immune system is a direct reflection of the character and deepest sense of this value . . . immunity protects that which is valuable. Immunity to the attack of pathogens is a direct correlation to the demonstration of personal wellness . . . wellness expresses valuableness over worthlessness. Some of the strongest immunity is found in persons with deeply diverse breeding. Just as the opposite is true -- inbreeding creates genetic weakness. Looking deeper into this . . . higher valuation generates courage; courage generates openness; openness will acquaint with strangers. Taking this to the most extreme cases in history -- archaeological studies of mating across deep genetic differences verify that there was tremendous immune benefits . . . still present in the today's DNA. When migrating "modern-type" humans bred with "archaic-type" humans, such as the Neanderthals, the innate immune strength of the resulting DNA improved. Science explains that Neanderthals lived in Europe and western Asia for 200,000 years before "modern-type" humans arrived, they were already adapted to the local climate, foods and pathogens. Interbreeding helped the migrating humans to expand their immune strength and meet the new challenges. Because infectious disease attacks weakness, the stronger genes involved in immunity spread rapidly through natural selection . . . they also spread their value of courage. You personally have these genes -- made possible by your ancient 'high-self-value' ancestors with courage -- not being afraid of seeing their self in a very different "other" person. Evolution always honors this courage of connection. Our prayer is that you make courage a priority in developing your path forward; take risks in ways that expand your views of what's connectable; also connect your views to the polarities -- to that which is completely different -- capture the reward of this massively increased value. Take the risk -- connect with those who are different -- evolution is now on your side of history.

The light-body is an actual three-dimensional event in our physical world. Nano-crystals within our body fluids are concentrated in the brain, heart, spine, hands, feet and thighs. These crystals respond to the pressures that yoga asanas apply to them and then increase their activities of alignment . . . receiving and broadcasting through their electromagnetics. Our prayer is that you know that this is real and then do the work daily to utilize these powerful connections.

*I*n every moment, every possibility is available . . . if not from the material realm, then from the massively abundant dark-matter, or pre-matter. These are the stem cells of matter; you open their possibilities by opening your beliefs, and reducing your doubts. With doubt, you will struggle, and push, and you may achieve your goals with great effort. Faith on the other hand, uses the leverage of your beliefs, employing the entire supply of these stem cells, to achieve your achievements with ease. Belief is always a mixture . . . it's your imagination mixed together with what you claim is reality . . . this forms what you 'believe' . . . is . . . or can be real. What this reality is -- for you -- then establishes another opinion; draws a new conclusion, and produces an even deeper belief. When life accelerates -- like it is in these present days -- the doubtful 'ancient evolutionary impulse' is always triggered . . . survival first. This survival reaction asks -- "Where's the danger?" Then, you add the accelerating social energy, thickening the pot of global pressures -- like the very nature of today -- and there appears to be more danger than ever before. Doubt will identify it all just to feel safer. The new evolution however, as opposed to this ancient survival mode, is the realization that there's always an equal amount of opportunity, to any danger . . . you note the danger, and you've found an opportunity. Knowing how to steer your vessel of life toward opportunity, while still knowing the danger lurks in the shadows, is the skill set of humanology and kundalini . . . the advanced sciences of being a complete and conscious human.

Our prayer is that you take the courage, each day, to discover the abundant opportunities that "lurk" in the shadows . . . right there alongside the dangers. They are related by the laws of nature . . . there's always a balance. Use the danger to locate your new opportunity, and the shadow, with all its danger, becomes your friend.

There are many ways to bless this world with your life and one of them is developing constant conscious interactions that build momentum with people of higher awareness. It's called living in the company of people of love and it inspires you to keep up and make yourself healthy, live happy and aspire to your abilities as a sage of holiness. Our prayer is that you are a champion of such relationships with people of love . . . they will return to bless you and everyone else on Earth.

Within the vast cosmos there's a recycling system that allows for matter -- that's been exhausted over billions, even trillions of years -- to be reconstituted, recycled and reintroduced into existence. Every galaxy has at least one 'black-hole' -- this is the recycling system's entry point. Through here, all exhausted matter is reduced to its sub-sub atomic form via the massive force of highly advanced gravity . . . gravity so dense that it can reduce our Sun to the size of a 'pea' before disappearing it into the 'invisible'. It's returned to circulation, still invisible, through a corresponding 'white-hole' . . . waiting for a new assignment as matter. It's the stem cells of matter . . . it's called 'dark-matter'. Astrophysicists are noticing the gravitational effects of a gigantic disc of this invisible pre-substance spread throughout this galaxy . . . the galaxy seems to oscillate in a wave pattern passing through this massive invisible disc every 33 million years. Ancient masters knew these stem cells of matter are assigned back into visible matter by the universal mind -- the same mind-source of all thoughts. As unmotivated, unconscious beings, thought just appears. But as an advanced, conscious-awareness, you access thought according to your belief . . . your knowing. When in this advanced state, your system operates at optimal capacity . . . you become a co-creator. This is a human being, actually being human. You can literally manifest stem cells of dark matter into material form . . . it's a miracle. An unyielding, unwavering belief . . . an unreasonable knowing that requires absolutely no reason to know what it knows . . . this, the ancient masters referred to this as your 'immortal authority'. Our prayer is that you begin at the beginning; work with your belief system; expand your ability to manifest the dream of being you . . . all the raw material is there for you. Later on you can work with miracles . . . the possibilities are endless . . . for now, be content to manifest calm, joy and fulfillment.

*B*eing carefree (care-freedom) is the art of being free in the moments of outside pressure . . . a dedication to the complete failure of being controlled by OPO (other people's opinions). Ignoring OPO is not an obligation to "carelessness" -- it's a devotion to valuing yourself . . . the realization that you truly matter. And in this way you will find that you respect, but, "do not care" what others think. Our prayer is that you transcend your moments of outside pressure by living a carefree life within the highest amount of self-realization and self-valuation.

*T*he strongest, loudest, most compelling voice in any room, in any situation, is always the 'voice of warning'. The 'voice of warning' requires little vetting to be respected; requires the least amount of actual factual nature to be followed. In today's world, the 'voice of warning' is regarded as the voice of "wisdom" . . . the voice of a strong "leader." For millions of years -- along the process of evolutionary progress -- the 'voice of warning' delivered life to safety. However, this 'voice of warning' does not deliver life to growth. Today is a brand new evolutionary era, and the 'voice of warning' is no longer capable of leading. It must be heard as another voice in the mixture of all information . . . not the most wise; not the most compelling; not the 'must-follow'. If humanity continues to follow this 'voice of warning' as the 'voice of reason' -- there will be no reason to grow, or to evolve -- only a reason to remain "safe" -- and "safe" -- to this new era in evolution, is a dangerous place to dwell. Today, this 'voice of warning' will speak of survival, but it's actually not survival, it is stagnation. Stagnation is dangerous because it will not promote growth. Growth is actually always "unsafe" -- it means entering into unknown options -- with untried, unproven opportunities -- to achieve unimaginable possibilities. "That's irresponsible," cries the 'voice of warning' . . . "You're being foolish and naive," it claims. Well, this is the reason why the -- 'Fool' -- is the very first divination of the ancient journey of Tarot . . . because it's foolish to begin a journey into the unknown, however, a fool remembers what's been at fault before and forgives it; always hears and considers the 'voice of warning' and proceeds anyway . . . consciously; always knows the failings of the past, and courageously continues as if failure is essential to learning. Our prayer is that you hear the 'voices of warning'; allow them to be considered, but not considered to be most important. Evolution would not be here without them, and for this reason you must honor them for navigating your past . . . they are not, however, able to navigate your future.

Lifting awareness through each chakra activates the higher mind. Each chakra has motive and reason to use kundalini energy for its particular task and then release it higher. This is its assigned purpose . . . your task is to work the process with grace and skill. Our prayer is that you apply your skills to raise the kundalini energy daily and live in the resulting awareness with grace.

There's reason for life; there's purpose in living . . . otherwise you wouldn't exist. You exist as a mixture of purpose with imagination, realization, projection, reflection, and re-creation . . . all sitting in a soup called 'now'. Whether your soup is chaotic, or calm, or loving -- is determined by how closely you live up to the realization of your unreasonable purpose. The reason it must be unreasonable, is that there's often no obvious reason to love . . . only now will your greater purpose tell you that love exists everywhere . . . always . . . and that's unreasonable. It's only this awareness of love . . . that will determine whether you experience it. You have purpose in loving, but you often find no reason to love; this is when you must become unreasonable in order to remain aware of the love that is everywhere, always. Life exists in an ocean of it . . . it's the only way for life to actually exist . . . the existence of this ocean. It's at the depths of your unreasonable-ness -- where you locate the tiny similarities within the chaotic differences -- it's in these tiny similarities, where you locate the connections; it's in these connections, where you locate shared purpose . . . and within this commonality, you're delivered to those peaceful solutions. Within peaceful solutions is where you experience the safety of clarity . . . in the sense of this safety, your awareness opens up to the love that is there, has always been there, and always will be there. Chaos generates all the problems, and problems separate you; being critical of problems is like watering a tree at the branches . . . deep watering the roots is far more effective. Deep watering the roots is like loving another person despite experiencing all their problems . . . the problems in their branches. Our prayer is that you take the time in every year that's here and now; hold your family in its highest place; expand your sense of the family tree to include more branches than you can reasonably imagine. Use this imagination to deep water the roots throughout your surroundings and experience the love that grows everywhere, always. It's unreasonable . . . yes . . . and, it's filled with purpose.

*P*rosperity is a cosmic constant; it's the presence of love in an ocean that all life is immersed in. Awareness of this immersion is all it takes to benefit from the wealth it contains . . . measured by all standards, not simply financial, but financial as well. Our prayer is that you swim in the ocean with all that you're worth.

A spider does not weave a web; a spider exposes a portion of the web that exists everywhere, always . . . its silk threads reflecting the invisibility to your senses. These webs are universal -- they have no weaver -- they've always been there -- suspended in every space. These webs are what manages and connects nature throughout the multiverse. Spider silk is amazing, it's a tensile strength five times greater than steel cable . . . greater than any "man-made" substance. The sheer nature of nature has always enchanted science; four hundred years ago science said it would conquer nature . . . not a good idea . . . since nature holds everything together. It was this very conquering attitude that seems to have demolished both Atlantis and Lemuria . . . and two other far older lost root civilizations here on Earth. You see, this planet has lived through many incarnations, just like you have. This current incarnation is 13.8 billion years old, that's just the age of the present "skin." Hundreds of miles below the surface of the Earth -- there exists the remnants of previous life "skins." Remember -- Earth shifts, spins and orbits within a universe, which is spinning within a megaverse, that's 4 quadrillion, 843 trillion, 640 billion, 316 million years old. There are countless megaverses within a multiverse so old and vast that you can't ever measure. The farthest object, visible with the naked eye, the Andromeda galaxy, is a trillion stars, a mere 2.6 million light-years away. This vastness is what the great master Guru Nanak described as -- Wahe Guru -- because then you realize . . . perception is a mixture of this vast "reality," plus the "fantasy" of your imagination. Actual perception fluctuates according to the levels and character of the imagination you include in your mix. Ultimately . . . it's all real. Working with the huge numbers opens greater possibilities; connecting these possibilities are the webs within the vastness. Our prayer is that you discover your web that has no limits; connect all that you imagine, and join your loved ones in this strength and inspiration; ride this web with all your commitments . . . and remain enchanted.

Time: this mutable, movable, variable event of the fourth dimension determines how you experience every other event in three dimensions. The angles and ways you work with time determine the very nature of your world in every detail. Is it a healthy, joyful world you're creating, or is it not? Your choice of choices relating to time makes this a yes, or a not. Our prayer is that you make the 'yes' choices every day and bask in the consequences.

*Y*ou can be the most talented musician of all time, but if your instrument isn't tuned -- no matter how well you play the chords -- the music will sound like noise. This is the same as it is with your human instrument, you can have the greatest intentions in any moment, but if you're instrument isn't tuned; if you're not tuned into the moment, your contributions, to the moment, will appear like just so much noise. The 'music of the spheres' is always playing in the background of all the noise on Earth. The great masters call it 'Naad Brahm' -- 'Shabd Guru' -- 'the sacred music of life'. They devote their lives to it, to tuning their body, mind and spirit up with it. It's the glue that holds life inside of time, essentially the connection between Heaven and Earth; between your body and soul. Mantra parallels this sound; that's the power of mantra . . . the duplication of this vibrational glue on a very physical, and extremely practical level. Mantra is not philosophy it is science. When you sing these sounds, you're increasing the bonding strength of this connection . . . the connection between your personal instrument and the universe. For this reason, a large part of kundalini yoga is mantra, tuning up the mind -- and the rest -- the postures, breathing and kriyas -- they tune up the physical instrument -- the body with the mind. Mind is called 'man' (of mantra) in Sanskrit . . . and 'man' also means 'now'. Woman or 'womb-man' is 'now' plus the 'womb' -- which means 'future'. The woman is the instrument of the 'future' within the 'now'. The man is completely tuned into the 'now' . . . that is . . .

whenever he has tuned his instrument . . . when he's in tune. Our prayer is that you tune your instrument before you go out to play with each day; enjoy the music that's playing around you, and compose your own on the spot -- to suit the spot. Play so freely that the noise of life fades into the background, and help everyone you meet to dance into their brilliant future . . . be a Pied Piper.

*A*ll life is forever . . . all life is immortal . . . all time passes and physical aging is a habit of time -- not of life. At the end of all physical life, there is never a need to resign to the outcome; there is however a need to transcend it. Transcendence is not something that comes from not caring about what is, it comes from being carefree. Our prayer is that you transcend life in the carefree mode of forever.

Traditional physics -- the way science describes the universe to itself -- is facing a major challenge as quantum mechanics and general relativity open entirely new perspectives within the old perceptions of "reality." These disruptive revelations ask you to rethink your notions of time, of space, and the world of the miniscule . . . the quanta. Spiritual masters, over the ages, have spoken of this quanta using a different word . . . maya . . . the illusive and fluid nature of spacetime. We now live in an era where spirit and science are merging their vast knowledge bases into a kind of coalition. Like the doctor who says they've found the "God-spot" in the brain, science is merging with this awareness of spirit. Science has always focused on developing mechanical and mathematical tools of logic, but their research is rapidly discovering that it can't confine itself to these methods . . . it can't neglect direct intuition, or unexplainable experiential anomalies. It realizes -- it cannot neglect the invisible parts of the universe . . . it cannot let its obsession with logic ignore the magic. Logic is the 'yang' while 'magic' is 'yin' . . . not the magic of a card trick, but the truly invisible and unexplainable forces that exist. This is a perspective of "reality" that's grounded in the capacity of your intuition to imagine the world. Quantitative measures of qualitative content, has always represented science and its essential understanding of this physical world. But, what if the physical world is not all physical? What if it is -- in part -- a construct projected from beyond spacetime? Like soul plus body equals life . . . logic plus magic equals reality. Relentless love is the engine that spirit uses to create this coalition . . . science, now noting this relentless force, will soon be able to map the whole ocean of life . . . the logic and the magic. Our prayer is that you pay equal attention to the magic and the logic in your life, for they are equally real; open your life to the invisible forces of relentless love and bless this world with logical explanations for all the inexplicable magic.

The tenth gate, the crown chakra, determines how time is related to and lived through . . . a system operated by the pineal gland. This is the gland that is in turn managed by the Sun . . . it's the solar angle, relative to your place on the Earth, that feeds you with time's messaging. Our prayer is that you relate to the Sun, even when it's cloudy, and allow the light to brighten your moments.

*B*less you in this Universe that measures time -- which is created by space in motion through a point of reference -- that
point of reference being you. Thoughts normally follow this
construct of time through these motions and call it the passage of time. This initiates a sense of mortality, which is known
as your emotions . . . emotions are attached to this illusion of
the motion of time. In every moment you have sensations, you
have feelings, you have stored emotions -- and then you have
interpretations that go along with every sensation, feeling, and
stored emotion. All of this influences your experience . . . it
all influences the pendulum of time. That's the nature of the
motion -- and because of this -- no single moment that you ever
experience in this existence is exact -- there's always far too much
moving information for that to be possible. Deep meditative
breathing holds the construct of time motionless and places the
reference point into your heart through the pendulum motion
of each breath you take. When thought becomes still like this,
it develops clarity and a greater understanding of the vastness.
Slow your breath down, and the swings of space moving become
broader; time becomes more inclusive . . . because of this inclusion, thought develops greater clarity . . . emotions become
more relaxed…life becomes intuitive. When life becomes intuitive,
the reference point of time -- that is you -- becomes a heartfelt base of total knowing. This is the ultimate nature of the
mind . . . to absolutely 'know' time without the motions of
emotions that disrupt this knowledge. Then you use your emotions as a tool, rather than being used by them as a fool. Our

prayer is that you use the time you are gifted wisely; learn the art and science of focusing and slowing down your breathing to let your heart tell you what time it is. This calms the emotions that are in motion around you; builds your skillset of stillness and uses these emotions as tools to intuitively live in the nature of your heartfelt times with deep clarity.

*D*eath is the death of the breath of life, but it is not the death of life. Life is immortal and the surprise of your life comes at the moment of death. It's here that you realize that nothing has changed, except the costume that you've been wearing (the physical body) all this time. Our prayer is that you are aware of your immortality throughout the course of your mortal physical life.

*E*very December 31st and January 1st are just another moment . . . fictional and imaginary as a new year. Persians have a New Year in Spring; the Jewish people have New Year in the Fall; the Chinese have one in early February; the Vedic New Year is Winter Solstice, when the sun is weakest, but only in the northern hemisphere. However, the fact that so many people are celebrating in a single moment is what gives the moment its power; gives the moment loft . . . the same loft that lifts an airplane, in this instance gives wings to the moment. New Year's Eve is such a moment . . . the loft of collective conscious focus gives power to your resolutions. Take advantage of this moment in which billions are celebrating. Three generic intentions or resolutions that are helpful to create: 1) more ease in your physical body and world; 2) more calm in your emotional experience in the world; 3) more clarity in your mental perception of the world. Something to note: the tendons throughout your body, give your body tendency . . . which means the way in which you normally sit, stand and move also creates the way you normally view, hear, smell and feel. Rearrange the way in which your tendons hold you, and you're rearranging the tendencies through which you receive the sensory information . . . this is what forms your opinions, conclusions and beliefs. Any change in your beliefs will change the way you actualize the moments of your life. There's an ancient yogic saying, "If you want to change the way you think -- change the way you breathe, and the way you hold your body and your hands." By arranging the 'tendons' in your body posture, you arrange the 'tendencies'

of how your physical body affects your emotional experience, affects the mental clarity of your entire experience. Therefore, a great resolution at the center of this New Year would be conscious posturing . . . like doing yoga. Our prayer is that every one of your years -- answers your prayers; provides you with the tendencies of physical ease, emotional calm, and mental clarity . . . to give your intentions and beliefs the wings that fulfill your needs and desires.

*Y*ogi Bhajan had a 'notion' and 'intention' that guided his entire life as a spiritual master. His notion was: "to be here . . . and . . . to be here, hereafter." His intention, which he called the pathway to his notion, was: "to inspire students to become great teachers that would become ten times greater than he ever was." Our prayer is that you take this natural evolutionary wisdom quite seriously and strive, with each breath, to become ten times greater than you ever imagined you could possibly be.

Yogi Bhajan had, what we musicians refer to as, an "interesting" singing voice. You know what that word "interesting" means in this context. When you ask someone, "What do you think?" . . . and they answer, "Well . . . it's interesting" . . . you know there's a lot of critical information being withheld. One day, a highly trained opera singer joined our ranks; she wasn't about to let this go by unspoken. She walked straight up to Yogi Bhajan and said, "You know sir, you sing off key." He responded, "No." We all thought he meant, "No, I didn't know that . . . but thank you for telling me." Not at all what he meant -- as we discovered -- he continued, "I sing my key; you sing your key. It's up to you to find the harmony in the differences between our keys." How like life . . . it's up to each of us to find the harmony in all of our differences . . . it makes total inspirational sense. Gregorian chanting was popular at a time when culture restricted what was considered harmonious to only what was exactly the same . . . unison and octaves. It took hundreds of years to reintroduce the harmonic third and fifth -- intervals that Pythagoras and Plato taught as healing harmonies. It took nearly a thousand years to reintroduce intervals that create harmonic tension, such as the fourth, the seventh, and the ninth. What it takes to be truly you . . . finding the authority to be whatever harmonic interval you need to be . . . singing your own key always, regardless of the reaction. Hear the harmony where there is none. See the similarity where there appears to be none. Be a peacemaker where there are none. Give yourself the authority to free your voice, and you give your life the freedom of self-authority and being 'you'. You're only held back when you question your authority to be your own key. Because, let's face it, the only difference between a person who can sing, and a person who can't, is a belief . . . every voice is unique. Our prayer is that you sing a lot . . . in your own key; find harmony in awkwardness, and believe in it; allow others to sing their own key and expand your sense of the harmonious to include the whole "choir" . . . "angels" will be grateful.

In the material universe, for every action there is an equal reaction. Then there are moments in all lives when it clearly seems that this equality and fairness has all but disappeared; that life follows a randomly generated, painfully unguided path. These are the moments that the wisdom keepers would relish and say, "bolt your butt to the ground," or to the mat . . . stretch into your body-glove . . . deeply pray . . . silently meditate . . . for these are the moments where the equal and opposite is an impending miracle. Our prayer is that when these absurd moments arrive . . . do just this . . . look for the miracles . . . they are right there.

S ensations are estimates; feelings are approximations; thoughts are word puzzles. What your brain does, when it's unable to explain what it is right in front of you . . . it improvises. It will try to make sense of any situation that has zero sensory input, or that has an overwhelming sensory input . . . it will make something up. It will try to explain the zero-sense with common sense. This happens when you experience a powerful gong in deep relaxation, or a large conch shell being blown in deep meditation. The vast overtones are mentally unexplainable; your brain makes up a story to compensate for the sensation that's incomprehensible, and or intolerable . . . often time's people hear celestial voices singing in the midst of the gong. Both an overwhelming sensory presence and complete sensory absence will cause this. A perfect example of absence is what the indigenous people of the 'uncontacted Mexica' call Taquatsi, the deep-underground, character-altering, blackness (detailed in my book, *Buried Treasures*). There's also a substance that science is experimenting with, called vantablack, made of carbon nano-tubes. It absorbs all the light that strikes it; it's the blackest of black. In both these situations they reflect nothing . . . you see nothing. There's no place on the surface of the Earth that's capable of this phenomenon . . . only deep space, the deep underground, and carbon crystal nano-tubes. Physical vision works by sensing reflected photons (light particles) from all objects; your brain uses this light to mentally construct the world you experience. When no light is reflected, and you're unable to experience the outside, you draw imagery from inside.

You call this imagination, but it's really always mixing with your physical sight. This is the nature of your senses -- they're not exact -- they're estimates; always compensating for lacking data with imaginary mixtures of opinions and conclusions . . . fables of the present. Our prayer is that you realize how fragile your opinions are; how -- not real -- reality is; relax your grip and allow your world to transform . . . transform into a world of your dreams.

*E*volution -- in order for it to evolve and work -- requires all things to be greater with each generation . . . otherwise it's de-evolution instead. Religions that follow a prophet or series of enlightened masters are bhakti systems . . . the worshipping of masterful, ascended beings . . . a very powerful system indeed. Our prayer is that you acknowledge the greatness of that which you love and worship and dedicate your life to evolving beyond your devotion.

Spirit is a master of 'multi-location' of 'super-positioning' -- a master of shape-shifting the illusion in which all Earthly matter uncooperatively struggles. It shapes the physical body; fully understands your existential destiny; has a map to all your assignments, and holds this wisdom in the background every day of your life. It's your super-consciousness -- your higher awareness -- the key to everything in your world. But, the moment Spirit enters the physical body; and you are born into four dimensions of spacetime's existence, you lose this connection with these powers . . . they're replaced by the compelling noise of your Earthly survival. Bridging this predicament -- reconnecting the ethereal and the material -- this is easy for Spirit, but the ethereal silence is no match for your Earthly clamor . . . your body's senses rule life until death. Then the immortal Spirit re-emerges in a field of endless opportunities . . . the same endless field you lived in all along. You see, you live in a multiverse, with its countless megaverses, holding endless universes, all offering boundless options and possibilities for you in every moment. Spirit has the keys to every option of inhabiting any one of these countless worlds in any life. Then, with access to quantum mechanics, it's also able to shape-shift your world of choice to meet any need or desire within each life. If only Spirit had a voice; if only you were listening; if only when you heard this voice you were inclined to surrender to its wisdom . . . then it would be your guide through this realm; be your connection to higher consciousness, your awareness of your immortal self. This is your connection to time beyond time and space beyond all limits . . . when you have such a relation, anything and everything is possible . . . even miracles. Our prayer is that you recreate this relationship with Spirit; recreate a relationship with this ethereal silence within the material chaos; follow the guidance of this silence and arrive at your purpose -- your destiny. Then, make it your job to teach others the art and science of living this Spirit-based miracle in a material world.

The light body is an advanced aspect of human evolution able to build fifth dimensional connections with the radiant body and create collective harmony far beyond anything imaginable in three and four dimensions. The Vedic texts explain how to do this, as taught by ancient masters in states of ecstacy. The three and four-dimensional measurements of this are so astronomically large, and infinitely old, that they will make no sense to modern science, no matter how sophisticated it becomes. Our prayer is that you comprehend these values with your magical heart . . . it will allow you to make sense of that which makes no logical sense.

*D*reamtime and meditation affect the 'super-positioning' of every particle in your world. The theta brain -- reached in dreamtime and meditation -- is a powerful influence on your perception. It's important to connect with this power before each day . . . reset the 'super-positioning' of your perception and your world. In order to get to the theta state you must literally "hack" past the psycho-emotional codes/guards of your limitations and indoctrinations. It breaks up 'group-think' . . . the habits common to you, and everyone around you, since before you were born. Meditation and conscious dreamtime; the technology of kundalini and kriya -- the coordination of your breath, your voice, your posture and your movement -- allow you to break old habits and establish new 'super-positions' of your psycho-emotional perceptions. Many old habits blind you to the clues and cues from beyond the three and four- dimensional world. You live in the three and four-dimensional world, but your 'instructions' -- so to speak -- these clues and cues -- to your success in each moment, come from beyond the moment. Here, in the continuum of space and time, there's no such thing as "past, present and future" -- there's just one big NOW -- one moment containing all. Meditation and conscious dreamtime allow you to enter this realm; to learn its language that communicates within and beyond -- the language of 'instantaneous coordinated understanding' -- those moments you've looked into someone's eyes, and you both 'just know' -- both drawing a common conclusion without words. These are the ways that Spirit communicates; these 'instantaneous coordinated understandings' were yours prior to this physical birth . . . you can still communicate with this 'Spirit' world. Our prayer is that you relax your focus on this three and four-dimensional world for a moment each morning; allow your meditation and conscious dreamtime to carry you beyond the false limits; draw on the cues and clues from beyond it, to guide your life within it . . . live life on this Earth, created in this heaven. Jesus did, Mohammed did, the Buddha did . . . every great master did . . . you can too.

We've been gifted this three-dimensional spatial phenomenon of Earth; a planet balanced with cycles of time by the sun, all the sun's planets, and the moon . . . this balance of time in space allows life to take place. The five elements: earth, water, fire, air and ether produce the movement of life within the spacetime balance. The tides move in our body of water; the fire digests our food; the turbulence of the air in our breath captures the vision of our future in the lens of the ethers. Our prayer is that you relate to all these permutations and combinations daily and show the gratitude that will cause them to serve you . . . your life then lived in its grandest form.

The quirky laws of quantum physics show the universe as a fuzzy, predictably unpredictable phenomenon. Reality is perception, plus belief, minus emotional interference . . . with belief being the strongest part of the equation. This equation is filled with miniature spaces and quantum 'particles'. These 'particles' actually exist in a state known as "super-position." They are located in multiple places simultaneously -- that is until they're "observed" -- until they interact with you -- then they're compelled to settle into one place. This, like many other cosmic operations, is invisible -- it's magical -- but also extremely practical. Even though this is invisible to your senses, it's actually "visible" to your 'higher-senses' of love, trust and gratitude. Not only is it "visible" to your love, trust and gratitude, but these 'higher senses' produce the good health that allows you to extend your influence. This is evolution at work, and archeology has found that whenever evolution worked with this 'super-position' phenomenon, it produced the opportunities for building communities out of the random nature of human wandering. Over the centuries and millennia, human gatherings and communities have spread this love, trust and gratitude, which in turn allows diversity to discover its unity. This process still continues, but not without resistance, and as we move beyond seven billion people -- toward eight, nine and ten billion -- this unity within diversity will become mandatory . . . survival depends on it. The invisibility of all this is an illusion (maya); it's hidden in the light passing through the crystalline edges of every atom . . . confused by the psycho-emotional attitudes of the observer. These attitudes produce pressure-patterns on the crystalline edges of your physical body, which in turn affects the light that directs your observation . . . this then affects your inclinations and conclusions. Our prayer is that your beliefs in love, trust and gratitude serve you -- by arranging everything you touch, hold dear, and stand for, into 'super positions' that succeed . . . remember it's up to you.

*M*any studies have been conducted by scientists showing that controlling your lifestyle can lengthen your telomeres (compounds in the chromosomes that affect the aging process) and increase your life span. Some of the lifestyle practices that clearly produce and maintain healthy telomeres are -- deep healing nutrition; good sleep; proper exercise & stretching; periods of relaxation, meditation and prayer; singing, music and laughter. Our prayer is that you take part in these medicines every day and continue to live young and long.

There's always been controversies surrounding the celebration of anything . . . its the constant law of 'equal and opposites'. It's a law of nature, and this law will never stop . . . opposites actually hold the physical universe together. The 'holy days' (holidays), Christmas, New Years, Winter Solstice, et al . . . they've been subject to this law ever since the dates and days were established. All that history and mystery ago -- there's been push back against the origins and the ongoing stories. To push against the push back, there have been stories added to one another . . . one after another . . . additions to keep the previous beliefs active and alive. But, what must not be lost in all of this is -- each story has a purpose and a process, built over the centuries. Take the story of Santa Clause, short for Saint Nicholas . . . a remarkable tale. Also known as Nikolaos of Myra, a 4th-century Christian saint and Greek Bishop of Myra, (modern-day Demre in Turkey). Nikolaos was the patron saint of thieves and if you had anything lost or stolen, you prayed to him for its safe return. At Christmas time, your friends would search the thieves' markets for your items (lost or stolen), if they found them, or something similar, they'd buy it and return it to you. The story was . . . it came from Saint Nikolaos . . . from Santa Claus. People often ask my wife and I . . . "Do you celebrate Christmas?" The answer is simple . . . we celebrate any chance we get . . . celebration is good for life. The word "celebrate" means to honor and inspire, and we honor the inspired life and legend of Jesus . . . a story of life that humanity can also be inspired by. Our prayer is that you too, celebrate as often as you can, every chance you get, honor life and story with all your heart and soul; keep the celebrations of life alive and pass them on, with all the inspired tales, to each generation. Find peace, love and joy this day and every day, and a very merry Christmas to you and to all that you love.

"Sassy" or "sass" is the freedom of vocal expression and swag is the freedom of expressive movement. When you use these two tools of human expression and do so without causing harm, you are a great compliment to God's expression of human existence. You need to have both of these to operate freely inside your higher awareness . . . here is where the active spirit flourishes. Our prayer is that you are full of sass and swag every morning when you finish your daily practice, for it will greatly improve the quality of your day and the quality of the day for those close to you.

There's an expression in religion and spirituality, "As above . . . so below." This refers to the connections that are all around you. There are worlds and universes inside and outside your universe -- there's the astronomically large, and the infinitesimally small. Both are somewhat invisible to your senses . . . not invisible because they don't exist, but because you're simply unable to see them. Some objects are made visible by using lenses -- like a microscope and telescope that view the light from the object. The wavelength of visible light is between 4000 and 7000 angstroms (one ten-billionth of a meter). But the atoms in the universe are thousands of times smaller than the shortest waves of visible light. There's no material on Earth, from which a lens can be crafted, that's capable of viewing this size of matter . . . it is "invisible." And also, every atom has an even smaller connecting crystal structure to every other atom; you are physically connected to everything. Crystallography is the science that analyzes the light transmitted, reflected, diffracted and refracted from these invisible crystal connections between you and everything. This all sounds mystical, but it's actually very practical. Even though you're incapable of physically viewing these connections, your human consciousness is aware of what your eyes can't see. Down within the subatomic electrons, protons and neutrons and beyond outer space -- when freed from the separations of all measure -- when you release your focus on the molecular visible world -- you can experience your connection with everything. The most compelling traps that keep you "blind" are slander, hatred, gossip, fear and doubt. When you engage your faith of knowing without any reason to know, you move beyond these traps. Our prayer is that you find the courage to release the blindness that separates you in this visible world; have faith in the invisible connections that hold us all, and embrace these invisible bonds. This will create a world that nourishes you and supports every form of life to thrive in . . . this will create a heaven on Earth.

*P*ratyahar is the state of conscious awareness that synchronizes your smallest parts with the total . . . connecting your finite being with the Infinite. The emotional sensation of this connection is known as joy. The common "noise" of all the social and cultural indoctrination is what influences the human psyche to lose touch with this total connection . . . a connection that's actually available anywhere and at any time. When you breathe consciously, you connect with your heart; it's within this connection to the heart that you learn pratyahar -- your connection to the infinite that's always available. Once you make this connection, it teaches you the ways of the heart . . . the most connected and synchronized organ in your entire body. The heart is the first organ to be created in the early embryo stage of life, and it's the last organ to stop functioning at the end of life. The heart reaches every one of the thirty to seventy trillion cells in your body in every moment; it pumps your blood through the 60,000 miles of capillaries in a constant flow of exerting to give, and relaxing in order to receive back. With each one of these exertions -- each heartbeat -- the heart delivers your overall "attitude" to the two million brand new blood cells that are being produced with each beat. This blood is known to the masters of pratyahar as the liquid of your joy. Our prayer is that you consciously practice deep breathing for a few minutes every day; connect to your trillions of cells and this production of millions of blood cells . . . include yourself in your 'self'.

Do this by realizing -- no matter what else is going on in any moment -- your breathing is the most important thing going on in the moment. Create a life that synchronizes with the total; locate yourself in the midst of the breath, in the midst of the liquid joy . . . in the pratyahar. Join your beats and always smell the roses.

*E*verything that is meant for you, will come to you, as long as you are truly you, and relaxed at being you. The way you know what is meant for you -- what you are meant to receive -- you will desire it from the depth of your heart with a clear, sincere, unemotional knowing. Many experience this; it's called a symptom of elevated awareness. Our prayer is that you elevate your awareness, locate yourself exactly, (where you are and who you are) deeply relax and welcome the gifts of life.

The central sun of this universe is just one of the countless central suns creating universes upon universes throughout the vast megaverse. And then, of course, there are countless megaverses in the vast nothing of infinity. This is the very nature of nature. Physics and math tell us -- there can be 'nothing' that is infinite if it is 'something' . . . because all things that are 'something' can be measured, and infinity cannot be measured. Therefore, infinity has to be nothing. Each one of these central suns is the 'birth-star' of their particular universe -- and when you recognize how very large this 'space-and-time' is -- then you're not impressed by any concept of measureable wealth or riches . . . the items that have been collected by those who collect. Collecting as a measure of value has only been valuable for a few hundred years of eternal time. The agricultural and industrial eras have produced and built more than we can use, which triggered "collecting" and "hoarding" in the primitive brain. "Having the most" became deemed as purpose -- but in nature, life shares; death hoards and collects . . . this is the cycle of true wealth. When you view your "collection" of anything, against this vast nature of nature -- you realize how fruitless your collection is outside your own beliefs. Then stop . . . ask . . . what are the mechanisms of your measureable beliefs? Are you holding or sharing? Did you create your beliefs, or were they handed to you by an unnoticed path? And . . . do you actually want them? It's liberating to establish your own beliefs that are totally yours; ones that align with, rather than competing with the world around you. Our prayer is that you set up each year to be a year of clearing and joy. Let your prayer be the answer to your prayers; the prayers in which you are 'you'. Let the massive central sun -- that gave birth to this megaverse -- that gave birth to your universe -- shed light on your prayers through the channel of your beliefs . . . that are truly yours. Your prayers will come true with the great wealth of this liberating joy.

They've done computer studies on the human physical body and found that with zero tension, pressure, stress and friction it's capable of lasting for 335 years. Therefore, the length and health of your life will depend on how successfully you manage your interferences and disruptions. In the ancient days, so many of the great masters taught the technologies of how to use these interferences and the chaos to pass through turbulence with dynamic confluence . . . a music that becomes your friend and your core energy. Our prayer is that you use the tension, pressure, stress and friction of life as your core music to move you through the turbulence to your dreams.

As we approach the eve of another new year, many people's intentions can take advantage of this moment's levity . . . levity caused by the huge numbers focusing their awareness, love and hope on a new chapter of life. You can sail on such energies of levity and opportunities of hope -- created by the sheer volume of human bodies celebrating in three-dimensional-intentional space, and their brains igniting the fourth-dimensional-intentional time. This produces the phenomenon of collective levity . . . moments and spaces that enthusiastically leverage and embrace new revelations, relations, and manifestations. There is a power in this collective consciousness; you can sail on its levity. If this seems unfamiliar, then you're paying attention, because this is the way through the future, not common in the present dialogue, but described in many ancient teachings. It's experiencing comfort within the energetics of a crowded space -- comfort that leads you to think in compassionate ways; of service towards others . . . ways that open current spaces with future hopes. There's nothing logical, or three and four dimensional about these practices, but they're certainly important in today's world . . . a world that's getting crowded. It's your physical bodies, birthing your emotional bodies, turning your brain-mind connections on to the blueprints housed in spirit . . . physical bodies celebrating with ease; emotional bodies celebrating with joy; mental bodies celebrating with knowing.

Our prayer is that you dive into this realm; learn the liberating languages that communicate beyond its three dimensions of space and the fourth dimension of time; learn to manifest the containers of next year now, and enjoy the joy of the collective joy. This is sailing levity . . . this is welcoming a brand new year -- in a very ancient way -- for the most essential reasons.

*I*n March of 1975, I was flying home to America, after three months in India, paging through a magazine in a language I could not read . . . a page opened. There -- taking up the whole space -- was a photo of a painting done 200 years ago, of a woman who had lived 400 years ago. It was Mata Khivi, wife of a great master . . . Guru Angad Dev, third Guru of the Sikhs. A voice inside my head that I'd never heard before, whispered, "Here's your wife!" When I got home, I framed the picture, and spoke to it daily. Nine months went by; I was in Florida for the annual 3HO Winter Solstice Kundalini Yoga Festival. Walking across a field, I saw a young woman setting up for a yoga class. The voice returned and said to me, "There she is!" Thirty minutes later, I was called over by Yogi Bhajan. "Hey, Guru Singh," he said with a big grin, "You're getting too old to be a bachelor. Have you noticed someone recently?" He obviously knew, but in the moment we agreed to speak later and to wait until we both returned home. Ten days later, I called him; he didn't even say hello, or how are you, he just asked, "Who is she? " I answered, "Guruperkarma!" I had discovered her name during the Festival. He replied, "Perfect, call her up and ask her to marry you." I did just that . . . she agreed . . . and that was forty years ago. This is a story of faith, of courage, a bit of foolishness, and a whole lot of destiny. Our prayer is that you have faith in your own inner voice; that you use your courage, listen to its guidance, and create a sanctuary for yourself in its wisdom. Allow it to guide you to your heaven on Earth, and invite others -- one at a time, for a very personal reason, or many at once, for the general good -- to join you in your celebration.

Conflicts between ancient survival instincts and the higher human nature are in a mythic battle on Earth right now. Ancient instincts were built for protection through the ages -- your higher nature is a new entry on the stage of life . . . here to give life a living future. Because technology and weaponry have become as powerful as they are in today's world, the polarity had to emerge; this polarity is your higher human nature. It contains the trust, compassion, and intuitive neutrality to counter the distrusting brutality. Surveillance, distrust and brutality block human relationships for the sake of safety, but for humans, safety achieved with this violence is the most dangerous place to live. Humans are social by nature, and being alone, afraid and violent are not human lifestyles. Remember, only carnivores with claws make good loners. When higher awareness successfully contemplates the dangers of life, no matter how dire a moment might be, you don't experience the continuation of the danger, you register the danger; then experience the opening. The laws of physics say there's an opening in every moment. When danger triggers ancient instincts, it becomes too loud and boisterous, it becomes the only event in a moment, and the opening disappears. It's like a card track, where you don't see the slight-of-hand, you only see the misdirection. With instincts, you don't see the slight-of-moment, because you're too busy being tricked by the danger and its misdirected violence. Our prayer is that you figure the trick of the instincts out; find the peaceful opening in each dangerous moment; discover the intuition of your higher human nature and experience life beyond the noise of violence. This is the future of life . . . this is the living future.

When you find yourself muddled in the middle of nowhere caught up in nothing, you are ready to grow because you're completely lost, and being lost, like all things in this universe, is the beginning of the opportunity for its polarity . . . in this case -- it's being found. The great masters would say that they deliver the strangest thing in the world . . . the sensation of living in essence . . . being lost in the center of existence. You mostly can't see it in the moment, you can't smell it, and you can't touch, or hear, or taste it, and when it's being delivered you have no idea if it's even been delivered unless you're lost in it. Our prayer is that you are committed to being found in receiving an infinite blessing of being lost in your center, and never question the value of what's being delivered.

This year is moving towards the Winter Solstice on northern Earth . . . this is the womb of the year. W-O-M-B (in Sanskrit) means 'future-now'. You're moving towards the birthing moment of your future now. You want to use this time -- a time in which the sun is at its lowest angle, the moon, because of this, is much more influential -- to realize the feminine power in everything. These are your more grateful attitudes, your most receptive positions, and your more intuitive abilities. This is why there are so many sacred days, for all traditions, centered on this time of year -- masters have known of the feminine magic this season contains for millennia. This is where the actual physical energy of the year is rebirthing itself, and this is a time that you sincerely want to take advantage of . . . get into your meditations; get into stretching your body glove, and make your resolutions come into life. Resolution is re-solution -- it's solving a moment again -- that's what a new lease on life, a rebirthing is. You are to solve your way through your life again . . . the solution of the re-solution of any old life dilemmas. Numerological meta-science shows that 'nine' is the answer of the prayer -- the answering down; 'six' is the prayer -- the reaching up; seven is the work to achieve the prayer; eight is the reunion with infinity, and nine is the gift of infinity answering . . . the nest of the future has the answer. Our prayer is that you make this time a wholesome and holy period of deep resolution, prayer and meditation; believe in the things that bring great joy; use the magic of this feminine time to manifest your life, and give birth to its many blessings.

*A*n effective way to express your love of life and grow beyond your expectations is to dedicate yourself to becoming even greater than that which you respect and admire. This is known in yoga as the path of bhakti . . . its effectiveness is stellar. It literally bypasses your fear of the unknown, of things new, and causes you to grow where you would have been afraid to even go. This is because when you worship greatness in someone else, you feel uniquely safe in their shadow, in this unknown space, for they are the measure that it can be done. You will even end up wandering into spaces beyond their achievements as you project that they must be able to do this too. On the other hand, if you determine that you can never be as great as they are or were, then their greatness has little value other than being an icon of worship. Our prayer is that you discover the safety of loving someone, or something that is an inspiration to you, and then using this inspiration and admiration as a guide to grow even beyond your limits and their example of greatness.

Value is what you must live 'as' in each moment; it's called presence -- it's not what you live for. Storing value for the future moments must never replace the valued presence you receive from everything present in this moment. Your greatest task in life is to maximize this value of your presence. Yoga does this by coordinating your movement, with your breathing, with your speaking -- all into a united team . . . asanas, pranayama and mantras all as one. This is what is capable of receiving the greatest value out of your presence . . . health and wealth. With this united-union (original meaning of the word yoga), you engage your brain into a lucid, theta state; your body becomes at ease with effortless efforts, and your emotions are transformed into devotions. This manifests -- this is true yoga -- the total union between all of your parts . . . being one with everything and unconditionally connected. When you're in this higher state, and any "s*#t" gets dumped on you, it becomes fertilizer for the seeds of your ideas. At the very least, you think bright thoughts; have a moment of forgiveness; you use words like inspiration and innovation, which lead to actually living in brighter terms. Sounds idealistic, but yogis have practiced and perfected this for thousands of years. They were the first ones to evolve past the pursuit of instinctual revenge and into this idealism . . . they found it works. Our prayer is that you make it a priority each day to find the fertilizer in your nasty moments; plant seeds with your presence; act in a lucid state of ease and effortless effort, and remain united with the true value of your ideals and your ideas.

The mythos-scientific realities of unified spacetime (unified as Einstein saw it from a perspective without relativity) are obscured from those who rely on only logic for verification. This non-logical angle of observation, called the 'galloping stallion' by pre-Columbian medicine people, requires huge faith and courage to become anywhere close to your belief. Once in your belief-system however, non-logic can access enough thought and feeling to power your dreams into your space and then into this moment. Our prayer is that you relax your grip on logic, float into sensations of unreasonable magic, embrace courage and ride the stallion . . . all you've got to lose is a moment, but the upside is finding forever.

Some events are lived out in your dreams, to avoid dealing with them in daily life. Other times you plan events in dreamtime, in order to live out a daily life of your dreams. Dreamtime is beyond these three dimensions of space and the fourth dimension of time . . . it's a rehash of past moments, or a window into the future. Both of these still and already exist, but fourth-dimensional time separates them into segments . . . dreamtime puts them back together. The brain is the vehicle you ride through all spacetime. Your brain uses five separate timing programs to work with this. High alert is the timing program at one extreme; deep sleep is at the other end. Deep sleep is called the delta state; theta is dreamtime; alpha is relaxed; beta is very active, and the gamma state, that survival mode . . . is the one on high alert. The further from high alert you are, the longer the program 'time-wave' in your brain becomes. The longer these waves are, the more information they carry; the more information, the greater your awareness of any moment. This is how the inner workings of the universe travel through consciousness and out into spacetime. The theta state is the longest wave you're able to work with while still alert, but this takes great practice . . . go with any longer wave, and your sound asleep. Lucid dreaming and deep meditation are both associated with theta state. In these conditions your brain is fully present; you have access to information unknown to almost everyone. Thomas Edison used this for inventing; Einstein and Tesla used this for discovery; great spiritual prophets, throughout the ages, have used this state to know the deepest "secrets" of creation . . .

those hidden from the daily eye. When life sits in the 'cross-hairs' of crisis, like it does today, it's time to access this vast information, for it contains answers to even the questions that have yet to be asked . . . it knows no limits. Our prayer is that you practice daily to access your own dreamtime; discover your 'buried treasures' of wisdom; find the gems that are needed in each moment, and live fully present for everyone . . . become the solution.

*H*uman life is an experience in magnificence when done with the courage to make mistakes. You are the only creature to consistently learn and grow from mistakes . . . other species often perish from them. Sacred texts define humans as created in the image of God. The word when broken down: 'hu' actually means light and 'man' means mind in ancient Sanskrit. A human being is a being with light in the mind . . . this light is your information, intelligence, insight, creativity, imagination and intuition. It infers a capacity beyond the response to immediate circumstance . . . to conceptualize beyond events, and to discover a path unfettered by commonly held limits. The miracle of being human is a miracle of the space you hold and the time you allow yourself to embrace the solutions contained in it. Our prayer is that you team up with this miracle of being light and take the human experience for the ride of your fearless life.

The cosmos is an elegant masterpiece -- an unequaled marvel, but when you think about it, you must understand that it's not your thoughts that you're thinking. You, in fact, do not have a mind, you have a brain. Consider looking at this brain like a two-way radio, it receives signals on many frequencies from one vast magnanimous station -- the universal mind -- then translates them and shares these signals as thoughts with others. Back and forth, on and on, this process continues. It's actually the mind of the entire universe; even the entire megaverse; it produces all thoughts for all reasons. Your thoughts are not personal, they're universal . . . all the way from the most auspicious to the most despicable . . . thoughts of all kinds, for all occasions. It's a sacred geometry, the system that assembles your thoughts -- a web that has no weaver -- it's the nature of what you call your mind, but it's not yours, you just borrow its thoughts, like everyone else does. The qualities, accuracies, permutations and combinations of thoughts are only as good as your ability to surrender in the ocean of faith and trust that this universe floats in. Surrender to this, and you are fully in tune, completely in touch, for when you surrender, you gain access, you receive fresh new thought, thought that applies to this very moment and all its issues . . . not old thoughts from previous moments that are rehashed and applied to now. That old thought applied to this moment is what stagnates in the world today; causes old grudges, broken ideas and bigotry to result in violence. It's not simplistic, but it's very realistic -- surrender to faith and trust; gain access to this universal mind; use the fresh thoughts to solve the real challenges of today with real solutions generated exactly for today. Our prayer is that you have this courage, the discipline in your heart to be this pioneer; to take the risk and receive these fresh thoughts that have never been thought before; develop the skills to express these ideas and pray for those who might listen to them. Create a brand new bridge to peace -- for the old bridge has long been washed away.

Revelations at the quantum level say -- atomic particles of matter are not real; they form your world out of potentialities, possibilities and beliefs, but they're not an actual fact, or a real thing. Behind all of this matter, this extraordinary material universe, there's an even more extraordinary consciousness -- this consciousness is what's commonly referred to as the intelligence of God -- shaping each moment. This is the same event from which humans are said to have been created. Taking on the contrary arguments -- that there's no higher intelligence that exists -- imagine -- every single part of your extraordinary human body and mind, completely disassembled and scattered in disarray; then a whirlwind blows through this space for fourteen billion years . . . what's the possibility that a fully assembled, ready to function human is standing in your shoes at the end of this storm? The answer is, "the possibility is zero." Such is the nature of your miraculous reality -- you possess this super-consciousness of God; the capacity to shape and assemble your world from beliefs . . . shifting the possibilities and potentialities of each atom of space, and every moment of time., You have access to that super-consciousness at the center of this multiverse -- giving birth to the megaverse -- that leads to your universe. You are that brightest light of evolution, and in this you have a responsibility -- the responsibility to use, not abuse your power; to lift all other life that was placed here on Earth to accompany your journey. Our prayer is that you realize the simplicity within the elegance of your assignment; recognize your consciousness is capable of this entire revelation; imagine a better world through the eyes of your higher intelligence and rejoice in this miraculous opportunity . . . reshape your world for the better . . . do this today.

*I*magine how long it took to harness the wind; to discover cotton; to learn how it could be spun into thread; to then invent weaving all the threads together, and finally producing the cloth of a sail. Tens of thousands of years were spent discovering each micro-step along the way. Discovery comes with conscious intent and also without a trace of consciousness . . . just an unconscious stumbling through time. Masterfully guiding any idea toward a final result is a laser pointer combined with the roll of the dice . . . guarantees and gambles. The process wanders thoughtlessly and, at times, quite thoughtfully along parallel paths, or intersecting confusions toward its final success. Our prayer is that you value each crazy idea you come up with no matter how absurd in may seem. It could just possible be a micro-step in the discovery of our next mode of motion . . . sailing on the winds of gravity throughout and beyond this universe.

The neocortex is an integral part of the mammalian brain; the most recent part to evolve. It contains four lobes -- frontal, parietal, occipital, and temporal -- each performs functions ranging from sensory acuity to conscious thought. Quantum science says that time is just space in motion viewed from a single, non-moving, point of perception. Conscious thought is this point of perception; without it, there is no time. As space moves through your perception, the space which has already passed through is called the past; that which is yet to move through your point of perception is called the future. But, if you look at it from a quantum -- a fifth-dimensional perspective -- it all exists at all times . . . it's just beyond your neocortextual perception. Intuition is the ability to perceive in this fifth dimension; to understand the topography of spacetime beyond the perception of a single point of space, and a single moment of time . . . it is super-conscious. Even though the neocortex has been a tremendous advancement within human evolution; delivered all of your inventions; made parts of your lives more beneficial and advanced . . . there's a drawback. This benefit has trapped you in the illusion of time -- of conscious thought; the illusion that the only thing influencing the future comes from the past. This completely ignores the invisible topographical map -- it ignores the nature of spacetime. Outside this neocortex, or perhaps within a portion that has not been discovered, or perhaps within a combination of its parts -- rests the power of your intuition. You have this capacity to see the topographical map -- the fabric of spacetime that surrounds you; to see the inclinations, permutations and combination of the 'future' . . . 'now'. You can hear them, see them, feel them, smell them, and taste them if you allow yourself to depart from the view of your neocortextual logic. Our prayer is that you have the faith in the cosmos to depart from this evolutionary advancement; return to the base of your consciousness; know that you know what's beyond your five senses and deliver a brighter future than comes from the past . . . deliver it now.

*T*he three-dimensional material world is a fractal equation that spirals into the form of fourth-dimensional time out of zero-dimensional nothing. The actual sensation of this space and the memory of time are the fantastic opinions observing illusional yet influential angles in the midst of an endless mirage. Think of this the next time someone says, "Let's get real." And then there's the realization of this four-dimensional science that understands we are only able to experience five percent of the mirage. The other ninety-five percent (dark matter and dark energy) are invisible to our five senses. This means that there's a lot more fantasy available if we are willing to work with our imagination and create more possibilities within the invisibility. Our prayer is that you truly believe that anything is possible and you have the right to produce whatever you can imagine . . . then, making sure it's benevolent, you become the change you want to see in the world.

When the migrations out of Africa began, the fork in the road was where Israel is today. There were those who turned left and ended up in the northern regions of Russia and Europe. Those who turned right, ended up settling in South Asia. When the ice ages came with relentless speed, those who were in today's Russia and Europe were devastated, their food sources wiped out . . . they resorted to hunting, killing and eating meat. In the animal kingdom, carnivores are the only ones who divide territories and protect them aggressively. The herbivores eat together, share land together without aggression. The Himalayas (the only major east west mountain range in the world) protected South Asia from the glacial advances. Those that turned right, all that time ago, were not disturbed by the ice and spent their millennia developing great knowledge, wisdom and sharing everything. This is where living food, the metaphysical sciences and fantastic arts were first developed. But because of the vast aggression that comes with territory -- carnivores have now dominated the Earth. In the aggressive times, of territory and individual wealth, life has been about being the greatest; competing with others; winners and losers. Now, in these new times -- in order to survive -- life requires being great; seeing everyone as equal to you and cooperating for a collective win. Everyone in the new times will need to be treated with respect -- lifted with the common tide -- held in highest esteem -- embraced with equality, not mechanisms of hierarchy. It's now known to climate scientists -- for all humanity to be fed, your diet will have to be plant based; your attitudes will have to be sharing and caring . . . not competing and fighting. Human success in the new times will favor collective health, and collective wealth, for all life on the planet . . . not just humans. Our prayer is that you are ready to depart from the old normal; take on your new role of a master teacher, and teach the ancient collective wisdom by example; embrace everyone and enjoy their accomplishments as much as your own. Be the change that's essential to thrive.

A fact of nature is that evolution will attempt up to 50,000 innovations in order to get to one of them that works. Another fact is that only '0.3%' of the world's population is able to experience and understand the most advanced stages of human evolution. It is incumbent upon you to do this responsibly, because in most comparisons involving humans, there incessantly develops a hierarchy and this we cannot afford. It only leads to common conflicts achieving nothing. Experiencing these radical edges of human evolution does not make you more, or better, or special, or anything other than responsible for the revelations, visions and innovations you are having. Our prayer is that you experience this '0.3%' nature of nature and rely upon its compassionate awareness to show you a forgiving pathway through the 50,000 bumbling's that every person and moment of evolution will produce for each working innovation to arrive.

*G*aia is this sacred planet -- it's collecting evolved ones to leverage and raise the younger ones . . . you are the elders. Each day is your starting point, not your assigned persona . . . it's up to you to discover your value. The new economics creates a world to thrive in, not just survive -- it's a system of recognizing this value in each opportunity, without attaching debt to the value. When debt is attached to value, it makes a beggar out of the value holder, and transfers the value to the debtholder, this does not enhance any opportunity, but produces wealth and poverty. It also creates a commodity out of capital, which then becomes the focus of life. Life is to be focused on purpose, not purposed by capital . . . it's about the ease of joy, not financial worry and disease without joy. In this sacred compassionate economics, capital is nearly invisible -- a medium of the faith and trust embraced in an exchange . . . a simple point in the value of opportunity, not the focal point. This introduces capital to cover exchanges of faith and trust; fulfill needs, and honor value. This is the role of money in sacred compassionate capitalism -- a system of public economics, not private hoardings; of cooperation not competition; of sustainability without vulnerability; of the greatest good, not the greatest stockpile. You are highly evolved; it's time to honor this fact, and teach what you have embraced in your mastery. Today's economy ignores the global needs. In 1900, nearly 90% of all capital was exchanged on the streets -- where it paid for food, clothing and shelter. Today, this is upside down -- only 20% of all money ever touches a hand on the streets -- the majority is hoarded in vaults and accounts where it multiplies itself to produce wealth for a few -- while over 20,000 children starve each day. Our prayer is that you wake up beyond the primitive instincts; promote compassionate capitalism to share everything -- everywhere; build a momentum in your own consciousness of generosity and abundance to leverage the value of life . . . and save lives.

*G*enius is a condition that is radical and in some moments ridiculous. The external reactions to the genius can produce a disastrous sting to life. A tough thick skin, or fluid illusory dance are required for the genius to cope. The tough thick skin versions of coping are the most common and also the reason why most of you, who are capable of genius, will either isolate in depression, or hide your gift from public view in an attempt at normalcy. But this only shifts or postpones the pain, because normalcy and or hiding are ultimately excruciating to the genius and to their inspirational revelations. Our prayer is that you recognize and embrace your genius, expect the resistance, and become that fluid illusory dancer able to sidestep the arrows of criticism and jealousy . . . then reveal your magic.

Thirty million years ago a population explosion began amongst the primates . . . the dominant mammals at the time. Over the next twenty million years, the primates maximized everything in their environment . . . the mangroves off the east coast of Africa. Then two and a half million years go by; this explosion has become so widespread that it caused a full-on crisis of resources . . . sounds very familiar today. Time moved much slower back then however, and this crisis worked with an unhurried clock in a far longer now. To solve this crisis, evolution reached for a new dimension . . . that's the nature of evolution. In order to open this new dimension, the primates stood up -- to see beyond the immediate space -- to locate space not yet occupied and to discover the resources in this 'third dimension'. It took four million years to master standing on two legs, and during this time the hands formed; the eyes shifted more forward, and the brain adjusted to perceive this third dimension . . . it all evolved into the world of today. Now, three dimensions finds itself overpopulated, challenged, frustrated and violently; it is over-using its resources in an all too familiar crisis. You need the next dimension beyond space and time -- the new 'standing up' . . . this one's within. It will mean raising the kundalini through the fearful levels of existing consciousness and into the fearless levels of the fifth dimension. This new evolution is the pathway into this next dimension . . . the answer to the global crisis. It was Einstein who said: "You can never solve three and four-dimensional problems with three and four-dimensional thinking. The three dimensions of space and the fourth of time do not hold the answers . . . violence will never create peace. You must solve the known problems with unknown solutions." Our prayer is that you realize you're able to lead this new evolution; you're an engineer of the next dimension; willing to stand up; ready to build this world into the heaven it is with your fearlessness, your sacred prayer, and your deepest gratitude.

*B*eing non-violent, non-judgmental and neutral-minded does not mean that you bury your head in the sand; do nothing and say nothing. Quite the opposite, it means that you are aware of everything and capable of understanding the path to outcomes without becoming upset, tense and aggressive. Your neutrality allows for a genuine curiosity . . . the angles and triangles that can alter any moment are revealed within curiosity. The non-judgment allows for a depth of understanding without violent defensiveness. The ancients proclaimed: "Have the eyes of a hawk and the heart of a dove" . . . awareness of everything -- clear knowledge of the pathway to guarantee benevolent outcomes. Our prayer is that you are so incredibly comfortable with your awareness that you see pathways to benevolence even when the path is cluttered with blockages.

The entire human body is filed with light (waves and particle/photons) passing through nano-crystals. These crystals, suspended in your body fluids, are all refracting, reflecting, magnifying and transmitting this light throughout your body-system. When placed under pressure, nano-crystals act as 'piezoelectric generators' and then produce electro-magnetic fields. These fields cause your individual body-system to interact and entangle with other bodies . . . your relations, your relatives and your animals. This is the force of attraction behind all relationship clusters and personal connections. There's a phrase, 'locality loopholes' -- it's used to explain the quantum speed of the relation between entangled light photons. No matter what the distance, entangled photons affect and react to each other 10,000 times faster than the speed of light. When in relation our light-bodies are filled with these entangled photons . . . we are forever woven together no matter how far apart, nor how distant the past, or the future. Our prayer is that you ride your light-body like an angelic force through the wilderness of life -- past, present and future -- knowing that you are always connected . . . knowing you are always affecting each other faster than the speed of light . . . forever.

*L*iving nature exists within a state of ease, joy, knowing and liberation -- allowing you to sail your vessel of life through the universal matrix of tension, pressure, stress and friction. The question is, which one of these do you usually experience? The stressful matrix is essential to all material forms -- it holds the universe in its suspended state of existence. Remember this on those days when the relationship between tension, pressure, stress, friction with ease, joy, knowing and liberation seems to be working dead against you. Above all, do not take it personally, for although the stresses are forever surrounding you, there's a sanctuary of ease within its very surroundings. Your consciousness is the doorway between them, your willingness is the key . . . time is waiting for you to open it up and access your joy-filled space. When you exert this willingness, you make the connection to meet the higher you within you . . . it is called being self-sensory. Our prayer is that you experience this sensation of higher self as a deep friendship beyond four dimensions, a friendship where ease, joy, knowing and liberation prevail. Embrace this friendship as a birthright . . . reach out into it . . . claim it . . . live in it.

The 'Uncertainty Principle', formulated by the German physicist Werner Heisenberg in 1927, states that the more precisely you measure a physical particle's position/location, the less precisely you are able to determine its momentum, and vice versa. This principle, often invoked outside the realm of physics, describes how the mere act of observing something changes the very thing being observed. How well can you ever really understand your universe when your universe is so changeable? Think about it, until your last breath, there is still breath; when there's still breath, there's still life, and when there is still life, there's a way to change everything that you observe. As long as your heart is beating -- (the heart is the home of the will) -- there is a way to change your observation. Therefore, "where there's a will, there's a way" is not a quaint philosophy, but this is the reality of quantum physics . . . at the core of your existence. Our prayer is that you embrace the uncertainty of your physical certainty . . . use this reality to produce your own reality from the dreams in your own imagination, and "become the change you want to see in the world."

*E*nthusiasm -- often associated with youth; at times connected to irresponsibility; then, experienced as overpowering, disruptive, or out of place in social settings. For this reason, there are cultures of "adult" age people who avoid enthusiasm at any time . . . "playing their cards close to the chest" . . . stagnating. All of this has given enthusiasm a reputation, sometimes good -- but often bad -- and why there's resistance and stagnation with the ideas and energies that are critical to solving today's issues. We have a world that's constantly changing, and currently changing at warp speed, combined with large sections of the populace that resist change. This polarity between how the world is naturally changing, and the unwillingness of people to enthusiastically embrace it, produces human stress and tension among the factions. When this tension reaches a sublimation level, the response is generalized fear, aggression and war. Enthusiasm is important in these moments because it's a great technique for moving stagnation by using its stress and tension . . . stagnation that's been unwilling to shift under any other influence begins to move. Enthusiasm -- when applied to moments like this -- can produce clarity out of stagnation, faith out of fear, and allow intuition to replace the ignorant noise of banter . . . a banter that leads to violence. The clarity and intuition that come with this enthusiasm, allow movement to open options before the outcomes are known . . . this is faith. It's faith in the unknown, and movement that doesn't have to be pre-approved in order to be allowed. Enthusiasm opens this faith and intuition. Our prayer is that you enthusiastically move whenever there's stagnation; recognize faith's advantage over every challenge; develop this movement without knowing the outcome and discover a world of options . . . then intuitively and enthusiastically make your choices.

*E*very creature's sense of time is radically different from the next, yet in fact, every moment of life is brand new. The only thing that carries forward, from one moment to another, is your psycho-emotional memory . . . some of which gets embedded in the physical body. It's known, however, in the theories and circles of high-energy physics, that at the quantum level of atomic and sub-atomic mechanics all of the physical world renews itself each moment as well. The knowledge of spiritual masters, throughout the ages, is that your consciousness can also reset itself every seventy-two hours. Whatever is carried forward within all of this equation, is simply the fuzzy memory of your fuzzy memory . . . you create time from the time you've spent and the only thing holding you back from your dreams, is a lack of memory about the nature of an equation. You see -- the key to an equation is that both sides are equal . . . the world outside is equal to your world inside. The question is . . . which side will you alter? Most people try to alter the outside one — this is arduous and requires a great deal of physical struggle . . . you can never really get to all of it, but everyone tries with all their might. This is the reason why money is so exceptionally attractive . . . it has become the leverage tool to alter the outside world. Masters, for thousands of years, have advised that altering the inside world is actually altering the source . . . the source code if you will. This takes radical discipline, but then you're built to embrace the radical natures of your moments -- after all -- you're a human . . . the fullest extension of the miracle of life.

Our prayer is that you are ready, willing and able to be human; to release fuzzy memory that creates the challenge of believing there's inequality in an equation; to order the outcomes of your desires with the clarity and newness of each moment; to be fully alive with your life and change the outside world by being the change inside.

There's a place between earth and sky that lives in your dreams . . . this is where your purpose lives and is accessed by hope, inspiration, enthusiasm and faith. Our prayer is that you dream big and enthusiastically keep the faith.

When you eat food, your body embraces the food -- completely surrounds it and takes it in -- digests and metabolizes the nutrients . . . eliminates the waste. When you energetically embrace the parts of any moment, you fully digest and metabolize the moment. When you metabolize anything, you absorb the benefits -- which are the nutrients -- then release the waste. Metabolizing a moment releases all of its debris -- all of the physical debris; even the psychic debris, anything you might normally hold onto . . . the toxins that emotionally poison you. There's an ancient proverb -- when translated it reads -- "Embrace the moment to erase and release the waste that would harm you." With this skill, you're living life at your highest level; your task is to then educate everyone else by example . . . not compare yourself to them; not complain about it . . . never fall short within its many challenges, but learn from it all and teach what you learn . . . compassionately. In order to accomplish this, each day will become your teacher; every challenge becomes your drillmaster. Approaching the time of life in this way, allows time to become extremely alive, for when you shrink from any moment -- for any reason -- you're shrinking from life itself. There are hidden qualities within time that are only revealed when you embrace, digest and metabolize them, just as there are unseen energies within food that are only exposed when it's digested. These are the energies of phenomenal power. When you ingest and digest this power in a moment, the moment is no longer the quality that your senses perceived; it's the qualities of these energies, the nutrients. Your system will metabolize the nutrients and eliminate the waste. With this hidden power, now digested, the nature of life -- which is miraculous -- becomes the nature of your life. Our prayer is that you will align with your miracles by living beyond what your senses feed you; ingest, embrace and digest every lesson of every day; release the distaste of the waste and live in your sweet power . . . the power of being the extraordinary you.

*D*id you ever look at a garden and realize that every color, in every flower, was made up from just dirt? No matter how intricate the color is, the only thing that creates that color is the dirt at the root and some water; the rest comes from the instructions in the DNA. All life is exactly like this, whether it's the life of a plant with a flower, or the life of you with your friends -- there's nothing in you except dirt and water . . . oh yes, and some fire, air and ether in order to stay alive. The only thing that actually makes any difference from you to your friends; from you to the flowers in your garden, to your cat, your dog, or anything, is the programming in your DNA . . . everything else is just dirt. Now look at the differences in DNA and you find that a fruit fly shares 60% of your DNA (your genetic instructions); the mouse shares 75% and chimpanzees share nearly 99% of exactly what makes up the physical part of you. What you're looking at here is, the only difference between one physical life form to the next, is the genetic instructions . . . these instructions are the DNA. The majority of life is directed and functioning under the exact orders of these instructions . . . how much of your life is genetic instruction and how much is choice, will depend on how conscious you are within each moment. The greater your consciousness, the more freedom you have to act on your choices. With this freedom you can choose to live at your center-point, or in your reactions. The closer you live to your center-point, the more you experience the nature of this center-point -- which is physical ease, emotional joy, mental knowing, and spiritual liberation. These are

the natures that actively exist at the center-point of all life --
plants and animals live here . . . what humans require to live
at this point is an elevated level of consciousness. Our prayer is
that you recognize the miracle in the colors of a flower; that you
see the direct connection between these colors and the joys in
your life; that you strive to be deeply connected and conscious
of all life, and celebrate this freedom with the colors of your
dreams.

*O*ne of the most profound 'other-dimensional' characteristics of quantum mechanics is 'entanglement' . . . two entangled particles will instantly affect each other across astronomical distances -- even light-years. This, faster than light-speed, violates a fundamental principle of physics known as 'locality'. This same phenomenon is also found in the properties of human consciousness -- human consciousness is not limited by 'locality' . . . that is, when you truly believe you're unlimited, you are unlimited. This is the power of conscious belief . . . in this case it's the non-local, non-limited capacities of your higher consciousness that belief gives you access to. Yogis and other spiritual masters, through the millennia, have proven that 'locality' does not apply to your higher consciousness -- or to the space itself around you. When you're operating in your higher consciousness, it appears that this fundamental of physics is not so fundamental. In these moments, the unbelievable and the impossible slip away, and in the presence of belief, possibility arrives; actuality reveals; the desired outcome already exists. Such is the entanglement of your higher consciousness -- it's entangled with everything, even beyond 'locality'. Our prayer is that you get out there; be bold; know that belief bends the flow of your world, like valleys bend the flow of a river . . . you are to receive the future and reach the "ocean." Understand the simplicity of this, that all moments of life are your opportunities and advantages. Take advantage of the opportunities, and find opportunities in each advantage you take . . . every point in space is entangled. Broadcast this belief across the astronomical universe, without a doubt for the distances involved; without concern for the time you have . . . and then -- faster than light in the moment -- there's no distance too far, and you always have the time you need.

*E*arly in the life of this vast megaverse, which holds the universe that you call home, the pre-matter was so extremely hot and dense -- "black-hole dense" – that it was only composed of sub-sub-atomic quarks and gluons in a plasma form, not bound together yet into the particles of actual matter. This was a state of total chaos, but it was chaos with a purpose, and out of this chaotic "soup" came all the elements we have today. Primordial chaos, that's still at the core of the megaverse, is the soup from which the matter of all life begins . . . into which the soul is placed. Such is the nature of ease, joy, knowing and liberation . . . the actual origins of life and love. In order to change your world, you must recreate this soup, and to do so you must recreate your awareness of the possibilities within the soup. It's a huge surrender, for this is the primordial mixture in which you dwell without identity. Without this surrender of identity and subsequent awareness, you do not advance, but simply lounge about life with the sole purpose of protecting an identity that is fleeting and temporal. In today's world, this is the state of total frustration at the core of all violence within the moments . . . moments spent in search of peace . . . the peace that is already there in the ease, joy, knowing and liberation, but invisible to your frustration. You, and this entire process are so incredibly sacred. Within your physical body (a temple), you have the only system that can re-present this . . . it's your conscious awareness. Actually located, non-locally, your conscious awareness registers locally in the system of your brain, nerves, thoughts and emotions. When you combine this system with a conscious will – 'will' is born within the heart -- you find the peace you're searching for; achieve the greatest good, and advance the love within the purpose of your life. Our prayer is that you break from lounging about, protecting the temporal identity, and re-surrender to capturing the momentum within your greater moments; ride the waves of this momentum for a while without any purpose -- then locate a purpose at the core of your will . . . right here in your loving heart.

*T*elescopes and microscopes have changed the view of this universe, from the time they were first invented, to the modern day of a Hubble space-telescope and CERN's Large Hadron Collider. These instruments give you an exact view of the world outside of the world inside . . . the so called "let's get real" view. Meditation is also an instrument of accuracy; it can discover the universal balance that prevails everywhere in the outside world by mapping the world inside . . . the real "get real" view. Meditation discovers the balance in a world . . . upside down without any upside. To view this hidden balance, you must first allow the actual moment to arrive within the upside down moment that's obvious; embrace even the most radical nature of any point in this moment . . . this is the core, at the core. Next, within the greater stillness that exists at this core, load up your heart with the calm and deliver it. Then, completely relax, for you are about to receive what's always going around -- now it's coming back around -- from your heart to your heart. This is meditation in real-time -- certainly not "wu-wu" . . . definitely "gets real" -- and you can do it with your eyes wide open. This is the power of your instrument; the gift of your imagination; the dream of your dreams, for when you completely relax at the core of your core -- you are who you are -- who you could be -- who you can be, or might be; your guide is anything that stands between you and around you. This is truly a "get real" moment . . . because this is the core nature of 'real'. This is your meditative mind as a telescope, as a microscope, as an inner-scope; this allows you the most accurate view of any moment. You see . . . the old phrase, "let's get real" -- was actually -- "let's get fooled and believe it." Our prayer is that you develop the skill to use this instrument of you; telescope your mind and discover the miraculous nature that often seems far too distant; microscope your heart and discover the love that surrounds you and usually appears too faint; become the instrument of your imagination to reveal your reality, and as the wise masters say . . . be the you in you.

*L*ife mimics a trail through the woods; there are trails that have been paved and thoroughly traveled; there are ones that are gravel and often rough; then there are many more as mere ruts in the dirt -- some faint, some well-worn. The more adventurous trails often barely show up -- many others don't exist until you blaze them yourself. As with most trails in life, and on a hike through the woods, you don't -- in any single moment -- see clear to the end goal. A certain amount of knowledge is required to reach this goal and a trail guides you with knowledge, step by step. Every trail and each step has a purpose in life; a trail cannot force these steps, only offer up choices. Steps and choices either run away from, or toward life . . . desperation and tension, versus inspiration and cooperation. There's abundant examples of how this works -- the mycelium serves the forest as the forest serves mycelium; the forest uses the land as the land uses a forest; the forest supports wildlife as wildlife supports the forest; the branches accommodate each other, as do the root systems. At times the roots do more than accommodate, they connect and attach one tree to the next . . . branch to branch, root to root, and breath to breath . . . each cooperation is a key to nature. It was 400 years ago when the scientists of pre-industrial Europe claimed: "We will conquer nature." It's exceedingly obvious throughout history -- evolution finds a way to extinguish any life force that turns against nature. Are we next? We fight everywhere -- nature produces everything. We must learn from nature that we're all connected at the root; we must accommodate each other in the reach of our branches;

what is good or bad for one, is equally good or bad for us all . . .
nature will always nurture those who are in tune with it. Our
prayer is that you go out into nature, walk on its trails, bath
in its forests, breathe in its rich air; open your cells clear down
to your bones; open your psycho-emotional bodies to as many
trails as you can -- cooperate from a place of being one with
these trails . . . walk throughout the nature of life.

There's a village in Africa, where, when a woman is pregnant, she goes out into the fields and forests; the surrounding areas -- she becomes silent; she becomes still and listens carefully; she hears the soul body of her child singing a song . . . it is here that she learns this song of her child . . . the one that has been with this soul forever. She learns this song and teaches it to her sisters back in her village. They all sing it throughout the pregnancy and especially during the time when the child is being born. This song welcomes the child into its life on Earth, and all throughout life the child masters the tones, melodies and words of this song. Within the dreams of its life, within all of its efforts and adventures, the child knows this song is there to move time forward through thick and thin. And when all the years have passed, the journey on Earth is nearly done, and time is passing from this physical body, all the village gathers around and sings this song as the angels collect the soul. This song has been with this soul forever and will be there forever more. Think about the nature of your song -- angels guide and guard you with this song within the wilderness of worldly ignorance. This is the song of wisdom, knowledge and magical outcomes -- of welcoming life on its journey through this world filled with cosmic surprises. From the sound waves to the nano-waves, you listen to the oldest and newest lights and sounds of this universe within the subtle senses of your highest consciousness. And there, you will always discover the nature of your song . . . it's powerful and phenomenal . . . it's the connection of the soul to the Earth. Our prayer is that you make every day, a day of your song; work with this music throughout each moment of life; collect the elements and implement them into your dreams and inspirations . . . be the one who sings when no one else is . . . be one with a song.

*T*ime: we measure it over great distances in light-years; we measure it through tiny sequences in nano-seconds, but it's actually neither here, nor even there. It's a convenient (de-con-fusing) perspective of a single moment . . . a moment standing timelessly still, while in perpetual motion. It's said that God invented time so that everything doesn't happen at once, and she invented space so that it doesn't all happen to you . . . that said, it actually is all happening at once -- and it is all happening to you. According to Einstein physics, time is space, playing and reflecting off itself as a space in motion through various points and angles of perception that are standing still right here . . . right now. It's a variety of perspectives within the same moment, strung together to create the appearance of motion. Great ideas dance in this stillness around your Earthly atmosphere, waiting for the angles of your dance, and the angles of collective perception to coincide. You see -- everything is actually a "co . . . incident" -- many things happening at the same moment, but viewed through individual and apparently separate angles. 'Creative-minds' -- with the courage to manifest their dreams -- consider every obstacle as a propellant within these fantastic realities. They chant the mantra "Keep Up" and they are kept up until the outcome comes. Like a massive game of cosmic gyroscopic-roulette, the wheels of time and wheels of perception counter rotate through endless gyrations, waiting for you to rest in the pocket of your gratitude. A wise dancing master once said, "Everybody wants change, but they just don't want it to be different." Our prayer is that you welcome the constant change; find comfort in your creative perception; embrace the dance and have the time of your life, believing in the value of your differences and thriving in it all right here . . . right now.

*H*ealthy wisdom acknowledges that human nutritional habits today, are generally abysmal -- the tongue is making most of these choices . . . "For two inches of the tongue's pleasure, you're giving up five to six feet of delicious health." His Holiness, The Dalai Lama once said, "There's no such thing as a 'fast food', you either 'fast' without food, or you eat food. In fact, food is healthiest when it's used medicinally, not as an entertainment . . . you really are what you eat. And the tongue is a lousy decision maker; as medicine, often the bitter foods are better for your health -- your tongue would never make such choices. Another side of taste -- the healthiest body is an alkaline body -- the tastiest foods however, are the acidic ones; the tongue chooses taste -- your discipline would choose health. Think of this as it relates to other habits and patterns in your world . . . life usually unfolds along the lines of your thoughts, emotions and impulses, but the healthiest influences on your life are quite the opposite -- they're your discipline, your points of focus, and your stability . . . all guiding you far more effectively. A human uniqueness is the free will, but in today's world it's not so much your free will that dominates, it's the lack of focus that mimics free will, and rules an undisciplined, unfocused life. Developing focus and discipline with your food habits can enable healthy longevity . . . but living in the grasp of your food impulses -- that delivers tongue pleasures with health problems. Evolution honors wellness and strength; when these are your values of choice, the taste buds will actually alter their preference toward health over entertainment. Remember, when you don't have your health, you don't have anything, and when you have your health, it reflects on every other part of your life. Our prayer is that you put health first; build your life on healthy choices with disciplined habits and a focus on nutrition . . . give yourself the ability to walk healthy, happy and holy through life, while creating your heaven on Earth.

Will and courage are aspects of the open heart, exposed within the openness and discipline of life's moments. Today is not a time of 'will or courage', 'openness or discipline' -- it's a time of 'sheer determination'. There's no compassion in 'sheer determination' . . . only achievement. And so we find ourselves living in a time of sheer determination with accomplishments and achievements . . . no compassion . . . no openness. This is a moment of evolution -- like a cancer's aggressive growth -- without regard for the life of the host -- our determination is producing accomplishments without regard for life. These are masking the purpose of life . . . people wandering toward achievement without wondering about consequences. This is evolutionary masks in place, hiding the pathway of life, all within the nature of balance, but we are currently out of balance, and must remove these masks -- remove these disguises entirely. And as these masks are coming off, we're viewing characters not exposed for centuries, on both the positive and the negative. Who are the characters of life . . . who are you? It's always the aggressors getting the running start in evolutionary situations . . . the mild, peaceful, more enlightened ones are caught smelling the roses. As this exposure takes place, things heat up . . . you are about to discover who you are. To be truly open and fully willing within your courage -- you must ingest this moment, before the moment arrives -- without knowing what the moment brings, but knowing that you know. Out from behind these times; out from behind these masks -- someone is emerging with the will and courage to dissolve the collective challenges. No matter how radical and awkward you feel -- your assignments in these moments are the keys for life to enter its next moments. Our prayer is that you take a pledge -- start today -- little by little advancing your radical nature with will and courage . . . accepting this beyond the awkwardness and fear; knowing this truly is . . . "What on Earth you are doing . . . for heaven's sake."

*D*ream about an epic journey: the most exalted of your many dreams; the journey of believing in your extraordinary self, and doing so for outstanding reasons -- the Earth's survival; a benevolent peace; the future of the children's children, and all because you have the innate ability to be a pioneer; a forward scout of evolution; a leader, a seer, and a master of lifetimes. Every clue to the map of this journey is buried deep in your own higher 'un' conscious . . . you've accessed them at times through your life, and though the messages are always faint -- you've known them all to be true since the day you were born. On this journey you've never really fit in to any "normal" -- "logical" setting, and the only times you were truly miserable were when you tried to. You did try often growing up, until you didn't, when you realized you fit perfectly into you . . . a realization that set you free. This epic fantasy is -- in fact -- your reality; it's your highest destiny; the classic mythic tale of a seed that's growing and repeating. You have an abundance of friends on this journey, but every one of you feels somewhat alone . . . a common thread connects you to each other in your own ways . . . the connection increases with belief. This is the journey that inspires you to rise up early in the morning -- to do the "let's get real" drill of opening your higher awareness with a daily practice . . . stretching, walking, breathing, meditating and chatting with those in love. This is the journey that causes you to eat right, so as to think straight, within the crooked path of life on Earth. It's the journey that allows you to "get real"

because so little else is . . . knowing you have to walk into this world each day, and be absolutely real, because when you're not real -- you're not you -- you're miserable. Our prayer is that you're determined to be connected to this journey -- this dream; determined to be exactly who you are -- ready, willing and able as the hero of an epic journey known as destiny . . . determined to be real.

*F*orgiving is letting go -- giving this moment forward into the next one. When you don't forgive, you hold the moment . . . you don't move forward. A part of you is stuck in the sounds, tones and images of a moment that's becoming the past. This attaches in your psyche -- where it will control you from the past. Forgiving is a self-ish act -- it involves no one else but you . . . you within your own moments. Releasing -- no longer attaching to them -- releases their 'ish' (their sting) from the self. It's accomplished like exhaling makes room for the next inhale. You literally breathe life out and in with each full breath. Moments move instantly to the past; noise becomes harmony; a completely new and unknown moment enters the 'now' from the 'future' . . . this is all for you to master. Life becomes about walking into the unknown -- mastering it; walking into the next unknown -- mastering this one . . . on and on. Such is the natural path of evolution. But humanity -- as of late -- has not been emotionally evolving, it's collectively lost the will to enter the unknown for a very long time. This is why emotional life has stalled for 10,000 years, and when life stalls -- it stagnates. That's where we are -- stagnating so completely right now that we're swimming in our own sewage . . . figuratively and liter-ally. This produces the opposite of the foundational ease, joy, knowing and liberation of peace . . . it's an indolence that allows disease, misery, ignorance, and enslaving indoctrination to pro-duce war upon war. There is a solution -- a radical, courageous approach to time . . . forgiveness that is so instantaneous that it pre-forgives each moment before you even enter; forgiveness before the fact, before the act, and before anyone reacts. This fully engages the heart center, the center of your courage and will . . . your stability on the Earth. Our prayer is that you open up your life and find the courage of forgiveness in the harmony of your heart; listen to these tones over all the other convincing noise; move with this fresh, natural -- not stagnant -- movement of time, and allow your moments to become momentous . . . to make for an extraordinary peace.

*I*t's a time to open the mouth of time -- to recall life's sacredness and thank each day for life. The original Thanksgiving was such a moment in history, and the continuation of another history -- a history of misery . . . the misery of colonization and subjugation . . . it continues. No other species, no other creature has ever colonized as systematically as humans, and no humans have done this as aggressively as the pale-skinned Caucasians. Anthropology researched and searched for a relationship between the lack of skin-color and this aggressive behavior against its own species, and the studies revealed some dots: (1) Evolution makes, on average, 50,000 significant errors in order to get one advancement that works. (2) Pre-humans and humans have colonized and enslaved since migrations began. (3) Removing pigment was caused when northern migrations -- where the sun is faintest -- reduced essential solar nutrients . . . everyone started out dark in the equatorial sun. (4) Evolution made this change to continue absorbing vital nutrients. (5) Lack of pigment is actually a base-weakness that evolution used -- and it worked -- but there were side effects. (6) Base weaknesses cause aggressive reactions to eliminate perceptions of disadvantage. (7) Skin is the body's largest organ; when a creature feels weak at its largest point, it's vulnerable . . . humans compensated by developing tools, which evolved into weapons, to make themselves appear mightier. (8) Historically, weaknesses couple with aggression to mask all perceived vulnerabilities . . . the classic instinct. Our prayer is that you demonstrate your gratitude this Thanksgiving by connecting some of these evolutionary dots;

campaign for the collective realization that aggression and bias toward race, gender, sexual orientation, religious freedom and other freedoms, is the result of evolutionary moves, with tragic side effects. Give thanks for the beautifully diverse and colorful humanity and your opportunity to correct these errors with common sense, sacred gratitude and collective tolerance for all of 'everyone' and every "other" one.

When you first learned to speak, in the early days of your developing childhood, it changed your relationship with the space and time and everything else around you. You've been advancing these changes ever since that first moment of language. These changes have served you well; they've defined you in your space; explained your space over time; explored and navigated these four dimensions of spacetime within your ever-expanding world. But language also stole something from you -- something very valuable -- something you were masterfully using in your preverbal state. Language (which means gauging-a-depth) took away your ability to focus, without measuring or analyzing, beyond the objects in a moment -- it took away your ability to experience beyond time and space. These were your innate intuitive powers -- powers built into your infancy's higher awareness. Prior to verbal communication, everything around you was an extension of your existence; you were able to experience spaces with profound accuracy; this is the psychic power at the center of your senses; this is the power of oneness. With the introduction of language came objectification . . . everything became an object; your words constantly describing and analyzing it all in greatest detail. This produces the mental noise of disturbance, something you were not plagued by when you were non-verbal. Now your task is to reduce this noise of daily life, the noise that drowns out subtle signals from your intuitive higher awareness; these are the signals of hope and inspiration; the signals of experiential accuracy . . . signals that give insight to the blind in a world filled with mystery. Our prayer is that you master your language, but also master your ability to turn it off and be silent. When it's time to experience the accuracy of unemotional, undisturbed clarity, be able to turn on silence and achieve profound connectedness at will.

Spirit enters the physical body, diving into the womb, four moons after conception. Just as with the construction of a home, a family doesn't move in when it's just 2x4's and cement; they move in when everything's done. Driven by the One-Soul -- a consciousness, an awareness known as 'spirit' -- enters its completed 'body-glove' to journey yet another incarnation. Collecting sacred assignments and the will to envision the future -- it enters the womb. This word 'womb' is from Sanskrit; it means 'future-vision'. 'Man' means 'now & mind' -- womb-man (woman) is the future embedded within now. This consciousness (spirit) -- driven by the soul -- orbits the mother even before conception and stays with the mother even if there's a miscarriage. The ancient wisdom-keepers would say "Spirit can even cause conception, by making the two participants look really good to each other at a particular moment." Then spirit supervises the construction . . . making sure that everything is happening just right. At the end of the fourth moon, 112 to 120 days, construction is complete; Spirit puts on its 'body-glove' and begins learning the art-science of physical existence . . . fitting into itself. It's advised -- by the masters -- "Never try to fit in . . . you fit perfectly in you." Spirit has been without a 'body-glove' for some time, in between incarnations, it has to learn how it all functions again . . . the muscles to arms to fingers; the pelvis to legs to feet -- and so on. The fetus does this from the roots of its bones . . . yoga in womb. One thing about your body, it's made up of all densities; some very deep, some not at all; it's the electromagnetics of tension, pressure, stress and friction that hold it all together . . . this is controlled by the Spirit, the will, and the ego. Yogi Bhajan would say, "Ego is the glue that holds soul into body; 'will' is the center-point of your heart, turning the possible into the actual; Spirit is the conscious vision of what is possible." Our prayer is that you reach into your Spirit to find a vision for the future; follow this vision by willing your ego to produce a life that serves you and everything . . . relate wIth this often.

When meditation takes you into a non-logical state, don't reach back for the logic of familiarity . . . swim further into the ocean of the unknown and allow it to teach you something completely new and evolutionary. Our prayer is that you are a lover of adventures.

*J*ust as the early usage of fire for cooking increased the size of the pre-human brain, the development of 'new-fire' is increasing the size of your newest brain, contained in the heart. This 'new-fire' is the passion for mastery and connection found at the heart chakra. Ganglia (clusters of neurons) are the physical realities within the metaphysical system of the chakras. This is the logical side of a very magical and complex relay of cosmic signals. These signals connect your life to the larger picture of all life. Though science is still unable to measure this -- the fact is -- every living creature is deeply connected with all life on this Earth and beyond it. Just as it took the invention of the telescope to allow Galileo to discover that the Earth was not the center of the universe, it will take far more sensitive equipment, than is currently available, to discover these intricate connections that exist universally. There are constant signals traveling throughout the cosmos -- it's called the universal mind. Amongst this endless information, within these signals, are the exact messages directed specifically toward your soul-body exclusively. This is received by your heart chakra; it's to be used to master your life. In order for you to have a relation with this mastery, you must first believe it exists; then quiet the noise that interferes with its reception; ultimately tune into it on a regular basis . . . every day if possible. In this way your life becomes guided, rather than guarded; a product of mastery, rather than a mystery; able to draw, and then follow a map to your destination . . . your destiny. Now you can locate your life accurately -- rather than drifting on the waves, winds and whims of meandering time. Our prayer is that you find the passion to relate to this vast system of connectedness; discipline your life and tune to it daily; build the magical maps to be anywhere you wish, always. By believing in your heart, become a master of life . . . because at the heart of it all, you are.

The ability to control and manipulate fire has long been credited with the evolution of human excellence. An unprecedented increase in brain size, enabled by a significant increase in the intake of calories from cooking food, corresponds to evidence that pre-humans began using fire occasionally, about 1.75 million years ago. At this time in evolution, the most important person in a tribe or clan became the one who found and maintained the fire -- the 'fire-keeper' -- the new "prophet." Archeology says that the consistent use of fire began about 781,000 years ago . . . meaning they were making fire now, not just finding it. Evidently pre-humans used found fire for nearly a million years before they could consistently produce it. This new ability to produce, control and manipulate fire gave pre-humans greater power and versatility; their ability to migrate; cook food all the time, and stay warm nearly anywhere . . . ultimately it helped develop language because of gathering together around fires. The era of the 'fire-keeper' was changing; the 'fire-maker' was now closest to life itself. Again in today's world there's this changing of the guard -- the 'keeper' to the 'maker'. For thousands of years, it was maintained that only 'ascended masters' could grant access to the gates of "heaven" (your liberation). Such was the time of the 'fire-keepers'. Now, like then, there's a new evolution, the era of the 'fire-maker'; enlightenment/liberation is available to everyone . . . make your own "fire" – light your own light -- be your own prophet. It can still be bestowed; worshiping an 'ascended one' is a practice of bhakti . . . perfectly fine -- now you have choices. Our prayer is that you light your enthusiasm to be a 'fire-maker' -- never quench it; always look to light, warm, feed and serve yourself and everyone around you; discover that you have the innate ability and authority to be this prophet -- don't be shy, and definitely don't be surprised when you're criticized, or even slandered for being so bold and courageous . . . that's been happening for almost a million years . . . get used to it.

*A*s humanity slides into global crisis there is a real opportunity for evolution to awaken from its long slumber. That is what a good crisis is all about . . . an evolutionary stimulation. Our prayer is that you recognize these good signs in the chaotic times and default onto the side of growth and awakening.

It's true, everything you exist within, everything that makes up your physical bodies, and all matter around and within you, comes from the sun. Every planet and moon in your solar system is dust and debris from the sun . . . scattered billions of years ago. You are in fact stardust. Your bones have an even more special quality, they're made up of the oldest particles beyond this solar system; they've come from the suns, that have come from older suns, that have come from the most ancient suns ever. There's truth in the adage, "I can feel it in my bones." You live in a massive universe some 13.8 billion years old, which is tiny part of an even greater megaverse that is 2 quadrillion, 843 trillion, 640 billion, 316 million years old. This is in turn, a tiny part of a seemingly endless multiverse that holds countless megaverses, which contain universes . . . endless multiples upon multiples. Each one of these massive, ancient components gave birth to the next -- gave birth to the next . . . your sun is from a collapsing star, from the collapsing of older stars . . . debris travelling through vast quantities of time, over endless amounts of space. Your bones hold your physical form -- they connect everything in your body. They contain a center called marrow which produces two million red blood cells per beat of your heart; each one of these red blood cells carries whatever attitude is currently filling your being – the very moment that the red cell is made this attitude is registered. Imagine, your most precious messages – the fundamental attitudes of your entire life in this very moment -- are being carried by a cell made up of particles that have come from the suns, that made up the suns, that made up this sun -- not millions, or billions of years old, but quadrillions. Our prayer is that you realize the vastness of your being; allow this vast self-realization to register in your bones; give thanks for this ancient honor and share it with every living and non-living thing . . . after all, it's all alive.

For humanity to prosper and thrive on this Earth a second evolution is required -- this is the evolution of consciousness. The first evolution was the evolution of physical forms; this was completed 5,000 years ago; there's been a stagnation of human evolution ever since, within a pursuit of comfort. When a species stagnates there are toxins that arise physically, emotionally and mentally. This is why the human being currently faces such diseases -- look around -- no other creature has this challenge. We are polluting the planet beyond belief -- look around -- no other creature has this issue. Psycho-emotional toxins are deeply rooted in the causes of corruption, aggression, neglect and greed . . . all running rampant and posing as normal in humans -- no other creature has this. Clearing stagnation is an evolutionary mandate that needs immediate attention. This requires taking the risks that evolutionary efforts appear to have. Evolution doesn't play it safe, evolution plays it accurately. Remember: there are many views of every moment -- perception of risk is simply a comparison to "safety" -- a standard held in the angles and perspectives of the beholder. 'Safe' has been described by ancient masters as, "a most dangerous place to live." Risk with accuracy, on the other hand, is an invigorating environment to evolve with. Evolution is the risk with accuracy that uses environments to manage and navigate the tension, pressure, stress, and friction of nature . . . it draws people together around a common cause. Every living plant and creature is essential to this evolutionary equation and therefore every extinction of any life is a setback to the evolution of all life. Our prayer is that you focus all efforts to evolve your own consciousness beyond the personal need for comfort; develop a sense of community with all life as a primary goal and serve this with your efforts; take care of each other as if it's yourself . . . this formula will reduce stagnation, increase overall health, cause risk to appear as friendly, and guide life toward accuracy. This is evolution . . . it is essential now . . . join up together.

The two eyes in the front of your face can show you what's here in three dimensions; the clock in your mind can express the additional dimension of time . . . the eye of your spirit (the third eye) explains what you face beyond this three dimensional space, and the truth behind the stories in the time of your mind. The third-eye is one of the three fully formed centers of intuition; the key is not in having this capacity -- everyone does -- the key is in turning it on; knowing how to use it, and using it effectively. This provides you with a clear sense of compassion; the ability to know, feel and measure the true nature of your every thought, word and action. Atlantis, it is said, was devoured when their advancements in technology exceeded their levels of humane, intuitive, compassionate consciousness. When technology loses its compassionate purpose, it becomes solely the instrument of power, control and, at worse, potential destruction. We face these same dilemmas today, and have ever since harnessing the destructive power of the atom. It's the primary responsibility for those of you on the path of conscious-mastery to become a gyroscopic balance to humanity's current path; to maintain compassion in doing it; to remain on course in the midst of it; to act as an inspirational guide for the way people, cultures, religions and nations are dysfunctional, misinterpreting and rudely interacting. You must actually accomplish this faster than the speed of light through 'non-local' conscious focus . . . the deepest states of meditation and prayer. There have been monks and sages of every tradition, throughout every century, on every continent that have had this intuitive skill and responsibility . . . now it's your turn. Our prayer is for these ancient traditions of compassion to be cleanly mapped into your intuitive psyche; become a champion for humanity achieving peace on Earth; don't be shy -- know that you are one of the ones to accomplish this; allow peace to spread through every conversation you come in contact with, and care for all life.

Scientists working with bats have finally discovered their mechanics of landing upside down. It all comes round to inertia: when landing, the bat pulls in one wing and leaves the other extended so that they can flip over -- lift slightly -- plant their feet -- and land upside down on a surface that's above them. Far from getting in the way, the weight of their long wings is a key to these airborne mammals mastering this very tricky maneuver. How many times have you encountered the need to master a tricky maneuver in your world . . . a challenge that seems impossible to solve? Look again, because everything -- in every moment -- has a complete set of possibilities built into it . . . action-reaction and every angle (pointing toward the possible) in between. Look even closer, the solution must always be there -- it's the law of nature -- nothing exists without its polarity . . . not even the most challenging of challenges. Airplanes, phones, recorders, pianos, mobile phones, cameras, photocopiers, radios, televisions, violins, back flips, cartwheels and sky-diving, all appeared beyond reach at some point. What changed are the dynamics of belief . . . the events themselves remained the same . . . never changing. The evolution of belief is a progression -- first comes an idea, then comes its desires that build until their expectations produce a belief, or a doubt. Doubt is self-fulfilling, it can always stop progress, yet once there's a glimmer of belief, the knowledge and skill to succeed are at your fingertips . . . then it's just a matter of taking the steps. Our prayer is that you consider your impossible dreams to be the possibilities that are evolving, from their help-less birth, into a reality that's destined to fulfill their maturity. Look at every angle -- even the impossible ones -- build the inertia, for when you live with belief, you are truly on purpose. You can even "stick" your landings upside down and backwards if ever needed . . . like a "bat out of hell" entering heaven.

A human advantage is imagination -- the non-local, universally distributed system of consciousness -- your thoughts can locate anywhere you want with their ultimate distribution point being at the threshold of infinity. Wherever you are: you can daydream; you can imagine; you can project; you can reflect; you can focus right here, or anywhere. The closer you locate this awareness to infinity, the more leverage your consciousness delivers; the more power you can apply to change the moment. The greater this leverage -- the less any of the disruptive details can disrupt you . . . they have little power. It is said that, "the devil lies in the details," but with this kind of distributed leverage, you can use the details to sharpen your talents. The more these details are "infinitely" imagined within your psyche, the more cooperation from 'creation' takes place; events you desire occur with greater ease. The closer to the threshold of infinity you stand in your awareness, the more leverage you have to alter your finite life . . . eventually it's all changeable. This is the true nature of 'shape-shifting', where purposeful chaos un-shapes the 'un-wanted' in your world, to shift the nature of nature into that which serves you and others. Spiritual masters have practiced this for thousands of years, and now logical science is discovering the magical spirit. Quantum entanglement, one example of matter breaking all the laws of physics . . . twin pairs of sub-atomic particles invisibly connected through near-infinite time and space . . . faster than light. Molecular biology currently shows genetic messages transmitted (cell to cell) through non-logical and invisible modes -- 'transmission' (known since the discovery of the cell), has been joined by transduction and tele-portation. Now we're talking 'logical' science in 'magical' terms. Our prayer is that you cease holding yourself prisoner to the limits of logic; free your imagination into the magical winds of 'whatever' . . . allow John Lennon's messages in 'Imagine' to be a starting point . . . imagine your world in your own way. You have this right . . . it's yours.

There is far more wind than the amount captured by a sail . . . the remainder is the exalted power of freedom. Our prayer is that you recognize the power you possess and sail freely on its wind with every breath.

*H*umans have the most profound computing device on Earth . . . more powerful than any quantum computer . . . it can literally reshape life. The ancient masters, composing the Vedas, described within the illusion of maya, the 1,200 alternative intuitive perspectives, moving with every moment, on the wave of time. Each of these moments -- a single beat of your heart -- additionally produces 7,000 revolutions to this wave. That's a total of (1,200 x 7,000) 8.4 million alternate angles of perception within every heartbeat . . . options that are always available . . . always waiting to be discovered and used. This means that no matter how you first perceive any moment, there are actually 8.4 million other ways to view it. Many of these 8.4 million alternate angles give you greater psycho-emotional balance; others give more physical momentum; others insure you successfully riding the wave through tough times -- through normal moments of life. Learning to take full advantage of these alternate angles is a goal of higher human consciousness. First you must believe they exist; next you need to envelop/ embrace them with your imagination; then conceive, nurture and birth them for practical use. Envelopment is the mastery of belief . . . imagination takes away the mystery surrounding the illusion/maya . . . nurturing is the element of self-love and compassion . . . birthing uses the negative mind to endure all the accompanying challenges . . . the positive mind uses action to remake your life with the new events and moments and this delivers success. Even though 8.4 million is a large number, it's a finite one, and everything finite has degrees of predictability. It's within these predictables that you ultimate develop new habits and patterns . . . patterns within patterns within habits that use these new choices in ways never thought possible. Acting on these choices is a parallel world . . . a world of fulfillment. Our prayer is that you use the full power of your vast human computer; take advantage of this benevolent advantage -- the gift of your alternate awareness within every moment; balance on the wave of time and ride it to the time of your life.

Why, when searching for life on other planets, is water such a key to the search? Water is more than you can ever imagine . . . it is key to your imagination. In metaphysics, it rules the second chakra -- the center of reproduction (the imagined future); and the center of emotions (the power behind this imagination). The Earth's surface is 75% water; your body is 70% to 75% water; your brain is 90% water . . . water makes life possible. Water contains nano-crystals, they clearly display themselves when it slows down, when it freezes, when it freezes as snowflakes. Water is a tremendous conductor and carrier of electricity, our bodies and our planet are electric . . . they are electro-magnetic. Dr. Jacque Benveniste studied and documented the memory-capacities of water, which are the electro-magnetic qualities of the crystals within it, and the foundational essence of homeopathic medicine . . . a medicinal-memory. Water stores memory and then transmits it through your water filled cells and tissues. Water is also extremely forgiving -- it does not hold on to old shapes; when you she'd tears, you shed some of the pain of your old memories -- clearing the path for new joys . . . you can laugh so hard you cry, and cry so hard you laugh. Water forms the pathway for your intuition -- the more inclination you have toward this fluidity and change, the more your attitude has access to hidden solutions; your ability to transmit and receive answers increases and surrenders its fixation on any old dramas and traumas. It's all in the interchanging, crystalline nature of the water as you break down your rigid structure of memory and stored pain. Our prayer is that you allow your water to enable your flexibility; allow your flexibility to reveal your solutions; allow your solutions to create your future, and allow your future to appear in this moment -- to shine a light on and lighten the pain of your sorrows and the sorrow-filled pain of others . . . become the solution . . . become like water.

The origins of the quantum discovery lie precisely a century ago; in November of 1915 Einstein presented his revolutionary theory of gravity. You must remember that before and after this discovery and revelation, gravity was always affecting life in exactly the same way. There are many other massively mysterious forces within you and around you; they affect your every moment . . . yet you are not aware of them in any way. Before the world understood gravity, the Earth was thought to be flat. Until humanity understands these other forces, there will always be a bit of a flat-Earth of some kind . . . somewhere. Until you develop the senses to perceive, there will be realities you can't believe. Just in the simplest terms: dogs hear sounds that you cannot; butterflies see colors that you cannot, and yogis have taught of many forces, for thousands of years, which most people don't believe are real. As an example: you have an electromagnetic field, an 'aura' surrounding you, as does every "living" object in nature; this field can both transmit and receive information with other life immediately around you and at great distances. In order to take full advantage of this force, you must attune your subtle senses to detect it, process it, and re-transmit with it. All adventures into the subtle world outside of easily measured logic -- into the world of maagic (spelled intentionally) -- are journeys into the other half of the universe-megaverse-multiverse where our senses and our scientific instruments can't detect or define. There will be remarkable discoveries in this magical realm over the next few years -- discovering what has always been there -- but only now is beginning to be understood. This is the next 'age of enlightenment'. Our prayer is that you are open to learning all you can about this universe's other half -- the half that makes this a better place; to be inspired and use this knowledge for the benevolent advantage of everyone; to consider imagining miracles whenever you are stuck, to consider offering kindness wherever you feel you can't; to consider being considerate . . . always.

*Y*ou are not your body, your thoughts, or your feelings -- you're completely separate from your gene-pool -- yet you dive into it all and use it all -- your body, your thoughts and feelings within an ocean of physical life. Those gathered around you -- your tribe of relatives and ancestors (seven generations in all directions) -- plus all the ones you've gathered by choice and destiny . . . these have been waves in the waters around you for millions of incarnations. Your task, in any lifetime, is to clear this water of its toxic habits and stagnation. As you do this, it's also time to develop your inclusive consciousness . . . all while working your jobs, pursuing your dreams, raising your families, taking care of your lives. Whatever you're working out in any given moment, is either spirit-based challenge working through your incarnations -- or genetic based stagnation in your tribe and bloodline. Either way, it's up to you to clean it up . . . so remember, even weaknesses are/or have been strengths at some other time, in some other place. A hammer falls through a glass table in a moment of weakness, yet a hammer is needed to strengthen many moments. Always consider this when dealing with your tribal characteristics and weaknesses . . . always consider the blessings with the dilemmas in those around you -- be a lighthouse, and when it's cleared for you . . . it's cleared for everyone. This makes your world joyful, inclusive and under-standing . . . less critical and intolerant. It's the nature of nature; the collective evolution of evolution . . . let the universe serve you in the process. Our prayer is that you find great joy in the daily tasks of clearing the waves in your immediate world and

those in the oceans all around you. See your life with everyone in the same water -- in this way, when you clear your surroundings, they're cleared from affecting all of you . . . forever.
"Do unto others, and what goes around, comes around" are
no longer quaint, faint philosophies, but clear and purposeful
realities . . . for what goes around is definitely going to stick
around . . . all around, until it's cleared.

There's a strand of fear that weaves through every life in the fabric of space and time . . . ever present, even today, it can keep you clear, yet not fearful. Just as a pinch of salt brings out the flavor in food, this strand of fear is designed to bring out the reality of any moment -- separate the music from the noise -- define the opportunities in the obstacles. This strand of fear has been in the collective gene-pool of every bloodline for billions of years, guaranteeing survival for each specie within every challenge . . . a default mechanism embedded in the signatures of life itself. Today however -- after all these billions of years, and millions of incarnations, across countless planets in the multiverse -- the number of intersecting and interacting waves on the surface of spacetime has become enormous and chaordic . . . a little bit of order within a whole lot of chaos. Too many strands of fear have been cross-woven into the current fabric of every life. It is in fact an evolutionary trigger, for crisis stimulates evolution, but when humans are this consumed with fear and blinded by this much noise -- their awareness goes silent -- their consciousness numbs -- they become, in fact, dangerous. The current injustices and propensity for violence are a natural byproduct of these colliding chaordic waves . . . like sound waves compounding, your life rides the crest of these mammoth storms. Our prayer is that you ride these storms until they disappear (they will); ride them with confidence, skill and creativity. Untangle the excessive strands of fear that have woven themselves into your days; separate the noise from the music and sing a song that calms the storm . . . become an example for those less courageous to hold on to and follow. Turn this world into the sanctuary it deserves to be, with the life you deserve to live.

When Dr. J. C. Bose, living in India in the 19th & 20th centuries, studied the life force (prana) of nature -- he discovered a brain, heart and nervous system in plants; the abilities of metals to rejuvenate, and the electro-magnetic properties of crystals under pressure. He worked extensively with the electricity in crystals, and in doing so invented the very earliest radio. He discovered that when you put pressure on crystals it produces a piezo-electric charge and immediately forms an interwoven magnetic field. He began measuring this with his instruments and found that all elements were functioning as living bodies . . . animals, plants and minerals. This was also the first scientific proof of the aura, and it was not limited to humans or even animals. He worked beyond the edge of every accepted scientific belief system, here he found a rich, fertile realm for developing seeds of hope and thoughts of tremendous inspiration. He discovered that when he was surrounded by charged electromagnetic fields (auras) -- inspired thoughts occurred far more often. When he treated plants with positive thought; when he allowed metals in his instruments to have periods of rest; when he relaxed with family and friends -- these were the moments that were most productive -- most boundless -- secrets most discoverable. For the first time, science was proving what yogis had known for thousands of years . . . it was no longer "wu-wu" . . . it was measurable. This work proved that respect, love, understanding and compassion are amongst the attitudes that measurably nourish life. Our prayer is that you allow yourself to have time each and every day to wander out beyond the realms of common human belief; allow your thoughts to freely travel where no thought of yours has ever gone before; surround yourself by respecting and admiring everything around you for what it is . . . set up a field of highly charged electromagnetics and live and play at its center. At first you will be like a swimmer and stay close to the edge of the "pool," but this will change as you become more skilled . . . let it happen . . . give yourself boundless freedom in your ocean of life.

*F*raud factor: we've all felt like a fraud from time to time -- often for no obvious reason . . . it just happens . . . comes out of "nowhere." This has been going on in the human psyche for tens of thousands of years and there's a bio-evolutionary reason why -- but the reason no longer applies. Hundreds of millions of years ago, life was far more fragile; birthing and dying far more violent; taking care of the young more tenuous and unreliable . . . there were natural evolutionary rules developing in order for each specie to survive the ordeal. What science refers to as 'change-governance' was being established in the DNA of each specie to control the rate of change. Evolution was establishing how much change was acceptable and what was not. It was discovering (through trial and error) that if there was too drastic a change, from one generation to the next, the parents wouldn't recognize the offspring and they'd abandon it. Too large of an amount of rapid change was eventually evolved out of the process of adaptation over millions of years and all those 'change-governors' -- in control of growth -- are still in place to this day. This is why, whether you're climbing out of a hole in your life -- or up the mountain of your dreams -- or moving from where you are, to who you are -- there's a limit to the amount and speed of the changes that your DNA will accept in any one time sequence. When you exceed this so-called "limit" the 'change-governor' kicks in and the sensation sent throughout your psycho-emotional system is that of a fraud . . . it tumbles onto you with a dreadful feeling. This has plagued every spiritual advocate from Jesus to Krishna,

Buddha to Guru Nanak, and recently Mother Teresa . . . you are amongst esteemed company in these sensations. Our prayer is that whenever you grow rapidly (emotionally, mentally, and spiritually) and begin feeling like a fraud -- want to turn back and even hide . . . have the courage to "keep-up" . . . keep moving forward with the knowledge that you're doing something outstanding. You're setting off ancient evolutionary red flags and alarms . . . congratulations on your wondrous growth!

The human quantum crystal biology -- the phenomenal content in the fluids that make up 75% of your physical body, is mutable -- it changes according to the angles of lightness, and or darkness, in your overall attitude in life. You can even change this at will when your will runs deep enough. It's the magic that governs the non-logical nature of your subtle existence . . . the magic that influences the logic. In order to have any influence over this -- the very core of your being -- you must be a master of compassion and forgiveness . . . releasing the moments of the past that occupy any of your energy. This delivers your awareness to the clarity of a new presence, and builds from the brand new light that's shining through this fresh health. Without releasing the old stagnant moments, you hold on to their evidence which blocks out the new light in the current moment . . . the very presence of the present cannot shine through. Current moment -- also known as presence -- is the health that's within all new beginnings. Beginnings are made up of this healthy fresh light of brand new hope; of the insights and solutions to everything. The word solutions literally comes from this new fresh light shining through the crystals that are floating in the 'solutions' that make up 75% of your physical body . . . your attitudes shift the crystalline angles, which shifts the outcomes of the light. Our prayer is that your attitudes are filled with light; that you process your darkness rapidly and move on to the solutions that are waiting to be found, and use the magic in the logic to create a life of magnificence . . . live in your light.

*L*iving in the moment of every moment is the greatest form of health insurance and a daily practice of kundalini yoga is one of many paths toward this coverage. Our prayer is that you are fully covered in every moment.

There's an unusual evolutionary flaw amongst humans that Yogi Bhajan addressed once when he said, "Everyone grows old; very few ever grow up." We're very much like little children, but with a reversal -- where little children are often afraid of the dark, spiritual seekers are often afraid of too much light. Spiritual seekers will walk on the edge of darkness -- the threshold of light -- in order to maintain their sense of familiar identity. Deep in the light, in the brightest parts of your enlightenment, there's no shadow, no perspective . . . no identity at all. At this location you are merged with everything, which is extremely disorienting . . . you have to be at ease with being lost. Our dear friend, Maharishi Mahesh Yogi inspired the cover of the Beatles White Album with this perspective . . . as you recall; their faces on that album were devoid of any features or characteristics all that was there were their eyes peering through blank faces. This is the nature of the deep light -- uncomfortable to say the least -- comfort rides the edge of darkness, never losing sight of the familiar characteristics -- always relating as the person within a familiar persona. But enlightenment is completely unfamiliar; you move into an enlightened state without any of the known views; so far from the edge of darkness that you have no clue how to return to it. Our prayer is that you have this much courage; that you enthusiastically walk through the edge of any darkness; walk beyond this threshold of rules and embrace the 'you' beyond familiarity . . . the light-body of 'you' . . . the planet needs this 'you' right now to lead it out of its darkness.

There's a fable, centuries old, about a small community deep in a dank, dark forest. This village never felt direct sunlight; the trees were so tall and thick. One day a young village girl saw a butterfly -- obviously lost -- no one had ever seen a butterfly before; no one knew what a butterfly was. This was so enchanting to the girl, she began following as it flew through the forest, so thick that she often turned sideways to squeeze in between trees. Thoroughly enchanted, she kept following -- suddenly she reached the edge of the forest -- the butterfly flew into a meadow with hundreds of other butterflies, flowers and fragrances, and sunlight -- the likes of which she had never experienced before. So spell-bound by the deep comfort of warmth and the miracle of nature, she lay down to bask in it . . . to take it all in. The warmth was relaxing -- she fell deeply asleep and dreamed of this world she had never witnessed before. Late in the day she awoke; the sun was setting; the sky was turning all colors of yellow, red and orange -- she stood up and hurried back into the deep, dark, dank forest toward her village. It became darker and she felt lost -- eventually stopping to find her direction, but she could not. Afraid and alone, she rested for the night and in the morning members of her village, searching frantically, found her. She was scolded severely, and when she told her story, no one believed her -- no one believed there could be such a place of beauty and joy. They punished her for wandering off, and they punished her for making up the story . . . they simply could not believe in such a place. This is a story of those wonders in you, the ones you hold secret, the ones you're certain no one will believe. Our prayer is that you believe in your butterflies; that you follow them regularly; that you bask in their fields of warmth, beauty and joy; that you follow this path with courage when darkness seems to be everywhere. The meadows of your wildest dreams are just a butterfly away -- take time to observe the flowers -- smell the fragrance -- transform your dark moments into better moments . . . and be sure to tell others . . . eventually they'll get it.

Life dwells in an entangled environment, a web without a weaver -- intertwined and woven throughout this entire fabric of universes, mega verses, multiverses, wormholes, white holes and black holes building and holding the cosmos together. And yet you are not this experience -- it's all an illusion called maya -- it's not you -- and not your intuitive reality. Each moment's value is a place for you to be what you imagine, climb your mountains and make them sing -- or live in doubts that hold you to an imaginary lower limit. Einstein knew this vast environment and said, "Today's imagination is tomorrow's reality." To access your highest imagination, your highest intuitive reality, you must reduce the emotional noise, for emotional noise supports the illusion with its stories. Quietness allows for intuitive imagination to bloom. Everyone on Earth has a distinct emotional signature; each one has a series of default attitudes, emotions and feelings; some have a rapid fuse, and react instantly, while others have a longer fuse, and respond slowly. One style is not good or bad -- or better or worse, and no matter what variation of this you have and live with, it's up to you to learn how to set it aside, turn it down, and even off without repression. When wanting to access your true intuitive reality this is essential, and you have the capacity to dive into your core and discipline your emotional structure. One way to begin this is called 'forced-nostril' breathing. When you are stuck in a rut and need energy to free yourself; plug up the left nostril gently with your hand and breathe long, deep and rhythmically through the right -- when you are scattered and need focus, plug up the right nostril and breathe long, deep and rhythmically through the left. The left nostril cools and calms, while the right heats and energizes. You've been given your emotional signature in this life as a tool to accomplish your destiny and grow beyond your limits. Our prayer is that you take the time to discipline and work with your emotional signature as a tool; dive through the illusions and into your intuitive imagination; use this as a base to build your future and embrace your future now.

*Y*ou have lessons collected in your brain; you have lessons collected in your heart; you have lessons of great difficulty; you have lessons of great ease. All these lessons are produced from pure light passing through the lenses of perception, passing through the opinions of your history, passing into the mysteries of the future, while sitting in the presence of the present . . . producing the fabric of life that has no weaver. These inner lenses are identical to an insect's multi-faceted eye; you learned how to operate them during your thousands of insect lives. Where typical lenses focus light through angles, these lenses refract light, focus light using diffraction, bend light as it passes over the curves, reflect light, split light to divide it, multiply it, or disappear it. Each of these actions, in the neurology of your brain, is made from light and dark concentric regions calibrated for locating the familiar and analyzing the unknown views of your world. The distance between these concentric circles determines how far the lens can see through time and or space, and because they are flexible, this field of vision can be altered. This is the technology of intuition -- the altering you are achieving during your deeper meditations . . . hence why we call an altar -- an altar. It is said you must experience the world through the lenses of others; live the world through the lenses of your 'self'. When you want to truly understand what is going on with other people -- view the world through their lens -- all while living your life through your own. In this way you are paying attention to your own destiny while helping others attend to theirs. Our prayer is that you learn all of your lessons using all of your lenses; work with the unknown as easily as you work with the familiar; open up the fabric that has no weaver and alter your vision to readily achieve your mission.

The experience of your existence is a point of perception that began within your consciousness billions of years ago on the vast oceans of time. This perception has traveled on these waves for so long now that no one remembers their origins, but 'origins' are essential to awakening your consciousness. One simple law to remember, your origin is joy. Just as any paint of every color is mixed from the exact same white base paint, all feelings of any kind are mixed from the base emotion of joy. Any of your other emotions are just tinctures, and when fully experienced, will return you to the base of joy. All emotions are just colors -- the natural distortions of many layers upon layers of life, deposited into your consciousness over this base of your emotional origin . . . deposited over your joy. Every emotion tells a story of your vast journey, a journey that you now must travel through in order to reach the core of your being. The core is always there, it's where you originated from all that time ago: your emotional core is joy; your mental core is knowing; your physical core is ease; your spiritual core is liberation. The journey produces the lessons through which you must now learn with your life each day. Whenever you are living at the core of your being -- you're living in ease, joy, knowing and liberation. Your journey of this lifetime is the journey using what you've already mastered, to move through that which you have yet to master . . . one common phrase always applies here -- "Don't back up, severe tire damage." You will make mistakes, this is natural. Mistakes will repeat until you master the journey . . . be good with this. Mistakes are a sign of the courage it takes to master the un-mastered. Our prayer is that you are ready, willing and able to continue your journey to mastery; learning what you have not yet mastered, to master that which you've not yet learned; facing each mistake with love; knowing your life is a simple point of perception . . . perfecting this perception with joy, ease, knowing and liberation.

There's a superhuman opportunity in the current version of life -- it's a new evolution -- a new calculation for meaning -- a brand new era. It's your existence on freedom arriving at this opportunity in the midst of your higher awareness . . . it's the perfect storm. You can discover your place of no restrictions, at the moment of zero time . . . it's the threshold of infinity on the horizon of solutions before your eyes. This is the world of maximum freedom, you can go as far as you can possibly go while still in a physical body . . . it's magical. There's a map charting the details of this world . . . a world [not] the play of opposites, as all things have been in the past . . . a world not about competition, but of embracing compassion. This location of new dimensions is called the threshold of infinity -- the cross point between finite worlds -- the space not yet occupied, meets a time not yet existing. You enter when you take a perfect circle, or a perfect sphere, and bring it together with another perfect circle or perfect sphere -- there's no point of contact. In fact, contact is impossible, because contact would require at least a microscopic touching point -- a flat surface, and in a perfect circle or sphere there's no flat area . . . anywhere. These perfections are the confluence of your wildest perfect dreams; they produce massive turbulence in the space in between. There's never been so much energy for change -- a sublimation point -- a doorway opening into a new realm. At this point of no dimension, sits the seed of every need and desire you've ever known (past, present, future). Our prayer is that you take full advantage of this superhuman opportunity; build fulfillment into each and every one of your moments; use this phenomenal spacetime in the evolution of humanity to be the absolute you within the absolutely greatest you. Push back against all the push back, for this is your birthright.

The songs of your life are like fleece, a fabric from the trash of ancient ages. Fleece is the recycling of something that once served a completely different function in the past; now it has a new purpose, a brand new life -- like your current incarnation . . . a recycling of all your previous paths. You now exist as someone brand new . . . someone who serves the future of this present moment. Knowing this, you stand on the threshold of your constant cycle of birthing and dying . . . knowing there is no death -- no end -- just shifting, cycling and recycling. The only thing that dies in what's happening in any moment, is the moment . . . the 'what's happening' lives on forever. Beatitude recycles into new forms of beauty . . . beautifully. Like a matryoshka doll -- nesting inside of nesting, on and on forever -- one life inside the next. Life is treasures inside of trash, and trash inside of treasures. Forgiveness . . . giving yourself forward unto now -- a way to deal with every moment of trash and treasure -- is not getting hung up on anything . . . keeping the shift shifting. It's creating an exception to an exception, and then another exception to that exception, until there's an ultimate acceptance. Our prayer is that you accept the recycling of your cycles of life -- threshold unto threshold -- constantly reinvesting in the reformation of your information until you've refined life into your finest moment . . . the moment of exactly you . . . all right . . . right now. Know this, and enjoy your song . . .

*O*ver the course of centuries, the original teachings of mystical, experiential, and spiritual mastery, have been reduced to the rituals of ceremonial traditions. When an essential component of the human experience is removed in this way, the lack of essence -- something you intuitively know should be there -- creates a gap in the collective psyche. This gap stimulates evolution to fill it. The world traditions have responded with, "Let's get serious about what we're doing." And so it is on Earth here today, you have very serious attitudes throughout the rituals and ceremonies of these world's traditions, but clearly the mystical experiences of joy, revelation, awakening and connection are missing. These "get serious" attitudes -- believed to be the way by those involved -- are not the way, but their fanatic efforts weigh heavily on the lack of spirit. It's obvious to the youth that there cannot be a spiritual experience under such weight and so they wait for people like you to come along. This is your task, you are the new masters, reborn to teach the essence of the mystics and the experience of spirit. You have to withstand the deep criticism that will naturally come your way and cause you to stand out. The lack of spirit has produced an evolutionary crisis, much like the Renaissance period. This is evolution at work, and you are its hope and saving grace. You are being forced into your outstanding strength -- be at peace with this strength -- it contains a light force and this force produces an experience of spirit. You are the new mastery and the planet is counting on you to shine into the darkness with your example. Our prayer is that you make this renaissance a reason for your being; know that you won't ever fit in with most of what's around you; have the courage to be completely unique and outstanding -- the person of your destiny . . . quite odd, extremely sensitive, and unusually compassionate . . . the master that you are.

The grace of Angels in your life, the accuracy of all the guiding forces when you pay attention, and the incredible joy of your animals and the little children -- these are the benevolent remnants of your waves of consciousness echoing beyond these four dimensions and reflecting back with their great wisdom of 'life-in-now'. This is the example of all the very special powers that exist in this very moment, where there is no time and no three dimensional spaces. When these intuitive guides, events, beings and inclinations occur, you know that there's magic within the echoes. To achieve something here, you must believe and act as though you exist within this 'forever' and know that it's not a long time . . . In fact, it's no time at all. Your life requires the assistance of these guardians, these sometimes tiny guides and their light-body moves through your body's crystalline makeup to guide you from a space beyond time, and a time beyond space. This is why their presence feels so sacred -- never tires -- never ages -- never stops -- and keeps on going even after you pass from the moment. This is also the realm of your dreamtime which is why spending time around these sacred entities, angels, guides, animals and children feels so dreamy. Our prayer is that you call upon all your Angels; call upon all your higher guides in all their forms; call on them to rescue you from the illusions imbedded in your memories made up from other more fuzzy memories projected from within another story . . . that your angels and guides, in all their forms, whenever they arrive, guide you back into this moment; draw you out of past history and future mystery so that you can enjoy the joy that is always, always, always alive in this living moment.

*L*ove is an advanced awareness of what is . . . it is a cosmic con-stant . . . life dwells in an ocean of it. It is our awareness that allows us to experience it and to share it with our surroundings. Our prayer is that you experience the love that is always present and share it with all those who are present.

*E*very life on Earth has their physical body as an assignment to evolve consciousness through the vast trials of spacetime into higher dimensions of realization. You've been at this for millions of years -- all over the multiverse -- every life an opportunity to simply exist as your fate, or achieve this evolutionary goal as your destiny. When you fixate on the passage of time, the moments serve your fate, but when you connect to each moment's opportunity, time rewards you with the momentum of your destiny. Each crisis helps trigger this evolution; the current global conditions demonstrate that you've reached a major threshold. This is your destiny/opportunity standing right there before you. Stretching into your body-glove helps deliver this ability; breathing consciously helps deliver this ability; being mindful and compassionate toward your world delivers your presence and this ability to fill life with your presence . . . this is destiny. Stretching and breathing and compassion both inside and outside your body enables advanced electromagnetic fields (aura); produces biochemical movement (ease); creates additional movement in your heart, blood and lymph; stimulates the cerebral spinal fluid to create freshness surrounding the brain. This is why all animals stretch every chance they get, and why it's such a large part of yoga. When you accept each moment based on the story that has gone before it -- this is you living your fate. But when you gather your 'Self' together into this very moment -- in ways like described above -- now you have the energy to create your future regardless of the history . . . and this is you living your destiny. Everyone's destiny is bright and remarkable -- everyone's fate is just what it is. Our prayer is that you stretch into your body glove, breathe as deeply and compassionately as you can, and arrive at this moment with your full presence; gather all the vitality you are able to gather and present the gift of your destiny to those around you who are destined to do the same.

*D*aily life with memory and anticipation delivers opportunities of joy and upset on a moment-to-moment basis. The question is, which ones are you going to buy, which ones are you going to subscribe to, or rent -- even if you choose to not purchase. A true life skill is saying yes, or no to any moment, and to do so without ever feeling obligated, or guilty. This is not something to think about -- thinking travels through the channels of your preferences, and preferences are completely historical and future based . . . you want to be in this moment. To respond accurately to this moment you must understand this moment -- not tilted by the future, or tainted by history. This moment is the living moment and has everything you require to understand and respond with trust and faith, make a decision, and move forward. All of this can go on unnoticed, as if it's pure and natural. To naturally function like this, set aside time for a daily practice of conjuring up the experiences of greatness in your world; breathe this great sense deeply into your lungs; experience this viscerally -- feel it throughout your gut and chest. Keep breathing gently, deeply and experiencing this for three minutes each day. You are locking in a touchstone to unemotionally make those tough decisions from. Technically, within every moment, every 'thing' springs forth from nothing; this is the nature cause and effect. When you breathe and re-experience your greatest moments -- every new moment becomes an exposure of this vastness; the opportunities to be joyous are found living amongst the upsets, and the upsets are understood for what they are, or as Yogi Bhajan once told me, "Being upset is a set up." When you clear your moments, life proceeds with greater vitality . . . you are not being set up; your energy is not drained . . . all from deeply breathing your moments of joy. Our prayer is that you practice this on a daily basis and take on the opportunities to be upset as moments for understanding; use the joyful moments to sing, laugh, share, dance and prosper. If you're going to be set up, set yourself up for a really good time.

The Buddha would say, "Discomfort is my friend, for when I sit with it long enough, it will naturally turn into joy." In fact, sitting with any emotion, or sensation, is a skill of mindfulness, it drills down through the noise of any moment to get to the base of the moment . . . at the base of all emotions -- sensations of any moment -- is joy. All sensations are built upon this foundation of joy . . . this is the way the emotional body works. Every emotion is a direction, in the moment, on the map of your life; it can either be a direction that guides you, to move forward or back, or it's a pain that relentlessly chases you forward or backward. All of this activity -- when dissolved to the base -- becomes the base itself, which is joy. The most effective response to the guidance of these directives or pain is gratitude -- an emotional opening to all solutions. Like a guardian, an ally, or an angel on your shoulder -- gratitude watches over you in so many ways. It helps you to remain conscious to the smallest indicators in order to avoid needing the challenge of far larger and more disruptive ones. The universe is always an event of balance, when it seems to be out of balance, look for gratitude to direct you toward the whole picture, the larger view. Then also, whenever you face a very large challenge, take it on with gratitude, but do it in smaller pieces -- they will eventually guide you back to the natural balance. Our prayer is that you discover the discomforts and pain, disruptions and confusion you experience, are simply 'instruments' on the 'dashboard'

of your life, guiding you with their subtle and sometimes not very subtle indications toward the center, the understanding, the balance, the equilibrium and the joy of your life. Know this and be grateful for the guidance -- whatever form it takes -- and get back to joy ASAP . . . it's there waiting.

*H*igh power electron microscopes have revealed crystal structures in your DNA and many other crystal formations throughout your body, particularly the brain, spine, heart, hands and feet. They all transmit the light through your life -- extremely evident in the brain, where these crystals have formed mirrors inside lenses inside prisms; mirrors inside mirrors; prisms inside prisms; lenses inside lenses and on and on and on. The lengths and combinations of these permutations affect every brain, spine, heart transaction and thereby determine the nature of your thoughts, opinions, attitudes, and conclusions as well as your heartfelt dreams. The hands and feet affect all of this with your every action. In nature there are no straight lines except in minerals. Your earliest incarnations took place in this mineral kingdom as you learned to be solid and straight. Your final lives as mineral were as transparent crystals -- a world of total clarity and exactness. From inside your crystals comes the light of tomorrow, retained and transmitted through the moments of yesterday, into the time of right now. The beauty of right now is that it is right now . . . there are no other moments that contain any life. When you invest energy in the times that do not contain life, it's like fertilizing a stone . . . nothing grows. History and the future do contain key intuitive values however -- as the light passes through each of these stages, it registers the record of its journey . . . history becomes great learning and the future is not indelible . . . it can be guided. You don't erase history, but you can alter its impressions, which alters its impact on the present and future. You can erase future history and rewrite it entirely . . . all of this is working with light, and the course of light can be altered. This is why a place of prayer is called the 'alter'. Our prayer is that you work with the crystal-line course of your light; alter the course to suit your prayers with your mirrors, prisms and lenses; blend it and paint with it like the artist you are; design the life that your best dreams have dreamt . . . it's the crystal authority in your DNA . . . feel free to use it freely.

Think of these two common phrases: "What on Earth are you doing?" and another one, "Oh, for heaven's sake." Put them together and it spells out what's truly needed in this world today: "What on Earth are you doing for heaven's sake?" What are you doing today for tomorrow . . . what are you leaving for the children of your children's children . . . what is your forever plan? This is about destiny; about posterity; about the opportunities to contribute, to serve, to make a difference. When you use your pure intentions over your senses -- it does not pave the road to hell, but creates roads beyond your limits -- ones that are unlimited. You begin operating on this Earth for heaven's sake, where your life-skills fulfill their purpose; where your purpose is driven by passions; where your passion serves all living creatures and finds its greatest reward in doing so. One of the oddest and oldest predictions of quantum physics is that an atom can't change while you're watching it . . . this has now been confirmed in an experiment at Cornell University's Department of Physics. This explains why so many people lose hope while focusing on their problems . . . nothing can radically change under such a microscope. It's your time to overcome another flat Earth -- what to do, for there are so many flat Earth's to be overcome? When you begin overcoming these limited perspectives you are resonating with the ever-expanding forces of both the atom and the universe. With this state of resonance you produce revelations . . . revelations that design new motivations; motivate new planning; plan new worlds . . . worlds where greater purpose is not more work, but produces effortless effort. Our prayer is that you discontinue focusing on that which you need; on that which you want; on that which you think you need to want. Focus instead on the breath of your life, and how it creates the time of your life, one breath at a time. Find great joy in enjoying the joy of this person in you that breathes for your living with such effortless effort . . . focus wholeheartedly on the incredible world worth sharing with your children's children . . . a heaven on Earth . . . for heaven's sake.

In the depth of love, your inclination is to abandon every need for safety, every mechanism of security that you have. You're now open to "incidents" -- sometimes called accidents -- that naturally take place without motive; cause injury (physical, emotional or mental) without intention; develop misunderstandings without purpose. To be safe and secure in the presence of such potential mishaps, a normal response instinctually retreats back into protection, but protection lives inside a shell and also makes it impossible to receive love. Now you're in a trap -- living with love, but not in love is the expression . . . an illusion of painful confusion. A more masterful method moves away from protection and instead uses intuition and deflection -- a technique of angles, a very powerful martial type art . . . actually a material art, because of its skill for succeeding in the material/physical world. The capacity to deflect allows for security along with receptivity . . . you're not in a shell, opportunities abound, where protection would cut you off from the world. Deflection is a dance within every danger of the cosmos. In ancient history, deflection was taught as the dance of Shiva; the song of Krishna; the ecstasy of "I am Jehovah" and the serenity of Buddha . . . a state of total innocence dancing in the mouth of time. It doesn't cut off the world, but super includes the world within your highest state of receptivity. Deflection is the art of passing through spacetime, where there's no space for danger and absolutely no dangerous time . . . magical means in a logical meme. Our prayer is that you dance by yourself and dance with your lovers; abandon all protections and enjoy life as music; engage all the benefits that come with reception; deflect potential accidents; turn them into blameless incidents and enjoy the joy that causes no harm and no foul . . . because you can . . . and you are always in love.

Wisdom keepers have said, "The distance between you and your enlightenment is the length of your spine, and the time it takes to get there, is the amount you want it to." This may seem too simple and perhaps unrealistic to you, but if you think about it . . . all matter is energy reduced to an observable rate -- with each observation, the nature of the observed is controlled by the attitude of the observer -- time is space passing through an observation. Now ask the questions: What are you observing -- enlightenment, or ignorance? When are you ready -- now, or some future now? It's exactly the same as the difference between -- before you learned to ride a bike, and after -- before you learned to swim, and after. There is in fact no real learning here, there's simply a moment when you decide that you can -- because swimming is floating, which you can do without learning, and biking is balancing, which is the nature of the universe. Enlightenment is knowing that you know, and knowing that you know is believing that you have the authority to know. It's all in the angle at which you view your capacity and your challenge. When you view your capacity at the angle equal to your challenge, there will be no distance between now and whenever. When you view your capacity at an angle of difference, the distance between now and whenever will be as long as you hold on to the difference. The brain needs validation; it makes up reasons for self-examination; you establish the results against some future moment . . . the "moment" you decide you will be ready. Our prayer is that you give yourself the authority to be ready right now for what you are always ready for; that you know that you know that you are who you are; that you allow for the time that is reasonable and then become unreasonably capable of being exactly who you are at that time . . . ready, willing and able right now.

Tomorrow does not wait at the midnight of today in order to make its way into now. Tomorrow exists within every moment in the form of inactive potential. Our prayer is that you activate this potential and perfect your dreams, then revel in their fulfillment.

The struggle between gravitational attraction and universal expansion actually culminated around six billion years ago, this is when dark 'transparent' energy became stronger and a more dominant factor in the universe. Gravity is logical whereas dark 'transparent' energy is magical; there are other logical forces that balance this all out, because the total cosmos is in a constant state of balance. At that point, six billion years ago, any objects that weren't already gravitationally bound together — never would be -- and this set up the chaordic stage we live with today. Gravity pulls matter together, while universal expansion (caused mainly by the dark 'transparent' energy) constantly counters this gravitational pull . . . the constant play of these opposites established the opportunity for life to exist. The space around life must always be expanding . . . universes, meta-verses and multi-verses (that fill all space) -- ease, joy, knowing and liberation (at the core of every living cell) must bond together -- macrocosms and microcosms requiring constant expansion mixed with gravitational grounding. In order for your human brain to interpret and understand this expanding/bonding riddle (the third dimensional space right in front of you) you must be motivated and able to reach into it and use it. The early rotation of your thumb, to oppose the other fingers, gave pre-humans capacity and motivation to reach into the third dimension and gather food. The centering of your eyes in the front of your face gave you the ability to clearly perceive this space. Constantly expanding space allows you to grow your perspectives of opportunity throughout your life -- producing the psychic fundamentals of hope, inspiration and enthusiasm -- essentials for a healthy outlook. Our prayer is that you passionately grow your perspectives of possibilities; reach into and develop your relationship with the space all around you; take advantage of your psychic advantages as a human being and teach others to create advantages in their own lives . . . ground yourself in gravity . . . expand yourself in levity . . . build the world you dream of.

*F*or each evolutionary advancement, there are outliers that stand out because they are outstanding. They are not limited by the larger group . . . they are unique pioneers. Some of these pioneers have indicated ways to the future, while others indicated pathways to extinction . . . they were too far ahead of the times to survive. Before the primates began standing up seven and a half million years ago -- and then took four million years developing your intricate relationship between the spin, pelvis, hips, thighs, knees and ankles to remain standing -- there were pioneer primates that would consistently attempt to stand. Because this entire mechanism hadn't fully developed, they would ultimately give up the notion, but each attempt helped drive the progress of evolution forward . . . the outliers were ahead of the times . . . the times would catch up. When closer to the evolutionary completion of the mechanics of standing, the outliers -- these pioneers began feeling the strong drive. From the four legged, two dimensional world, the 'standers' began introducing a working relationship with the third dimension . . . the perception of depth as seen from their new perspective of standing up. Today there is a new evolution, a new standing up . . . the standing up of the kundalini and consciousness. Again there have been outliers and pioneers -- the prophets and messiahs leading the way on this path. They produced massive followings . . . now is time for the followers to mimic the master's "footsteps" -- actually stand in the ways they stood; experience the new dimensions they taught. Our prayer is that you discover the pioneering spirit of mastery within yourself; see the great prophets -- not as unique, perfect and unattainable -- but as perfect examples for you to mimic. Stand up inside your self -- raise the kundalini and experience the evolution of your consciousness. Follow the path of the great masters and prophets before you . . . they were definitely special, but definitely not unique. Know that you are equal and ready to follow in their great footsteps . . . our collective future depends on you . . . create this future now.

Yogi Bhajan was once told that he sang off key. He responded, "No, I sing my key -- you must be inclusive enough to accept the harmony." Melodies and rhythms make up the music for the dance of your life. The melodies are the notes that you find in your thoughts and ideas, and the rhythms are paying attention to the beat of your heart and the pulse of your breathing . . . this puts these ideas into form. When you combine rhythm and melody the masters called it 'naad' -- in ancient Sanskrit. It's the sacred nature of the song that plays through the pages of your story -- it's your life being written as a melody of ideas to the rhythm of your heart and breathing. As all of these songs are played, every one of you plays your own notes, yet the total composition is so huge, that it accepts them all. It's up to each of you to find the harmonies in the passages; to find passages in the openings; to find openings where there appears to be no opening at all, and discover the simplicity of nothing, where there appears to be too much of everything. This is the magic of your music, and it takes discipline, which means to be a disciple of your own existence, to keep on playing. You are that disciple -- allow yourself to produce, direct, sing and dance the songs that appreciate your existence amongst everything and everyone else. There's no escaping from the songs that matter no matter what you do . . . the music that matters keeps coming through, but when you ignore this music, that's where loneliness and suffering come in. These sensations are indications that you've stopped dancing. Our prayer is that you always listen to and sing the music of your life; dance at the core of

your song; hear the harmonies where there are none and help
the weary find their own song . . . be a 'Pied Piper' and gather
all the music into one giant symphony to believe, hope, live
and inspire all around you to sweep out the old -- keep up and
welcome in the new -- use the bold, while shedding timid and
shy . . . play with your own "key" and open the harmonies of
humanity.

*O*ur inclinations to fail and succeed exist within an identical 'want', but different angles of 'expectation'. You know what you want, but often don't know what to expect until you receive it -- then you exclaim, "I knew it!" . . . because somewhere inside you did know. Wouldn't it be wonderful to know what to expect before the moment and could guide it into existence, or out of the way? This is the power of intuition in prayer that can be developed by anyone who is human, and of course you are . . . humans all have the innate power to use the light (the hue) in the mind (the man) that makes you the hue-man (the light in the mind) that you are. This light, though it is everywhere, concentrates within the nano-crystals that gather where there are the most nerve endings. These areas are both the nerve ganglia that accompany every chakra, and also the seven areas known in metaphysics as essences -- the hands, feet, spine, heart and brain. This is why people have prayed for centuries by pressing their hands together firmly; sitting on their heels; bowing their forehead to the ground -- all of this posturing to produce the angles creating pressures in the body at the locations of these essences. This, the process of prayer, is a science of forces -- pressure within posture -- electro-magnetic energy propelling thoughts and emotions -- light directed toward expectation to produce mastery where there was once a mystery. Chaos is a natural mechanism of nature and a large part of the teachings of physics. Prayer works to shift and reduce, or exaggerate and focus these tensions and pressures of spacetime and use this chaos to disassemble and the expectations to reassemble the fabric . . . this connects your expectations to the impending manifestation and the rest is history . . . and the future. Our prayer is that you pray often -- as often as you think to pray. Pray in the ways that you've been taught and ways you know for your 'self'; pray on areas of your life that seem uncertain and pray on the ones that seem certain; pray for those you love and those you think you don't; pray to use the science of this logic to affect the science of magic . . . and above all, pray to expect success.

There is always nothing within every something, there is silence within every sound, there is calm within every storm, there is zero within every 'thing' . . . and when you add zero to any 'thing', it does not change a thing . . . not even slightly. At the same time, according to these -- the rules of quantum mechanics -- any 'thing' that is going to be, has to already exist; every 'thing' must be every 'where' in order for any 'thing' to exist any 'where'. This set of riddles is known as spacetime and when Einstein worked with this principle he said, "Today's imagination is tomorrow's reality." Wisdom keepers teach: before the sunrise of every day, there's an opportunity to establish your imagination for the day's reality. This is before anything else comes into your mind; before the time-waves of the day begin to stir up the waters of your life... a time of true communion with possibilities. Masters and wisdom keepers throughout the ages referred to this as the 'amrit vela' or the 'ambrosial hours' -- where the sounds of wordlessness comprehend the images in the silence . . . the intersection of reality and destiny -- where the prophets, angels, guides, and your own higher-self dwell. This is an arena of magic on the other half of this universe from logic. If we dominate our collective life with only logic, we are not allowing what could possibly be imagined -- to be experienced . . . we are only reopening what has already existed to repeat itself endlessly like some Groundhog Day Möbius strip. Our prayer is that you take advantage of this imaginary advantage (the future reality); every morning before the rise of the sun, imagine whatever you envision your world can become -- then expect these opportunities to arrive with the sun . . . if not today, some day; if not here, some 'where'; if not exactly this way, some 'how' . . . they're definitely on their way and you'll be here when they arrive -- for sure.

*H*uman beings are the only animal that is not instinctually driven when performing at its best. When a human being is performing at its best, it's intuitively guided. In order to support a life that is intuitively guided, you must have the freedom to make mistakes, for it is this very freedom to make mistakes, and not be punished, that opens the higher centers of the brain to intuition. Fear of mistakes shuts down your intuitive powers and turns on your instinctual patterns of emotion. In the mastery schools of the ancient past, mistakes were rewarded more enthusiastically than correctness. This method of education was training the student to have courage, a huge part of intuition; to have the courage of curiosity, a huge part of intuition; to have the freedom of fearlessness, a huge part of intuition, all to open up the higher centers of intuitive discovery. Mistakes were rewarded as indications of exploring the unknown, for you cannot venture into the unknown without making them . . . and a lot of them. Over the past 150 years of the industrial revolution, education has been created as a training ground for job placement, not the education of life's fulfillment . . . you've invented intelligence without compassionate consciousness. Today's world faces outstanding challenges -- challenges that have never been faced before in the history of humans; you require intuition far more than you need your instincts. With the advanced technology being invented -- technology that can destroy you if you use it incorrectly -- you will require the freedom of intuition in order to be guided and survive through the century. Our prayer is that you influence the education of everyone in your family and everyone you come in contact with; encourage the courage it takes to venture into the unknown adventures, to discover the previously unknown answers in the unknown realms. In this way you will create the freedom and strength to make rewarding mistakes at a personal level, and then intuitively discover the answers we require to survive at the collective level . . . surprisingly, these mistakes of great courage will allow all species to ultimately survive these incredible times.

*T*here have been major shifts and evolutionary trends throughout the history of life on Earth. Angles of diversion -- triangulations of position -- reshaping of trending patterns have been constants over eons that produce the variations we live and survive with. They sometimes work, and then sometimes they don't. Science says evolution attempts as many as fifty thousand variations in order to arrive at one that works. These shifts occur both inside and outside of life itself, and the outer development must be balanced by an internal revolution of consciousness -- otherwise the resulting disequilibrium produces a culture that's unworkable and unsustainable. Such are the historical estimates of what happened to several lost civilizations: Atlantis, the Anasazi's, and the Mayans among others. With Atlantis, for example, the leading estimates are that the development of high technology outpaced the psycho-emotional development of compassionate consciousness . . . the result was self-destruction. With the Mayans it's well documented: the over-use of local resources far outpaced the ability of these resources to replenish themselves. Today, you have the extreme potential of both these events happening simultaneously . . . the perfect storm. Technology (like the atomic weapons industry and A.I. development), coupled with the depletion of essential life supporting resources (air, water, soil and sustainable climate) is threatening to produce environmental, emotional and physical chaos on Earth. This is a blameless event -- no one sector is fully responsible -- it's a collective responsibility. However -- unless the compassionate natures, deeply imbedded in human evolution, can resurface and reassert themselves -- this imbalance will become overwhelming. Our prayer is that you take up the role of a responsible adult with this growing trend; gather as much momentum for the cure within your own personal lifestyle as possible; influence those around you, in a compassionate way, to do the same; create a world you want to leave for the generations to come, and make this your raison d'être.

Space and time arrived and evolved simultaneously as spacetime. Time is a perspective of space and space is perceived from within time. All arose from a single point of no dimension; now you and everything and everyone are still connected to that one point of original existence by the threads of expanding spacetime -- rays and strings that shine out and stretch out from this single source. Science calls this 'the singularity' and when you view each other through this single common point, you are not separate at all. Over the ages, the millions of years, you have isolated and perfected your individual images to such an extent that you've forgotten this eternal connection at source. You, and everyone, have given away great power to this denial of connection -- like a leaf on a tree that does not believe it's fully related to the leaf hanging next to it, or on the far side of the tree. This sense of separateness gives rise to all of your negative emotions, the ones where you fear another leaf, doubt another leaf; believe that other leaves are your enemy . . . or at least not your friends. You share the same roots and trunk, you are the same life-force and whatever happens to another -- definitely affects you, even when you're not aware of it. Every other piece within the entire "tree" of this universe is connected to you; maybe a connection long forgotten and disconnected, but trace the entire threads and it's you. When your consciousness comes to realize this, you can leverage the knowledge and power of the total -- when this leverage is used benevolently, it is wisdom. Our prayer is that you begin developing this awareness right away, and use this wisdom to connect each and every person you meet to each and every person you meet; that you discover the similarities amongst everyone and find the threads that connect you to these shared aspects. This will relax all your base emotions of separateness and activate the crystalline genes of creative non-reaction . . . the most powerful solution oriented imaginal genes in your entire physical universe . . . this is truly you being one with everything.

You do not have a say, moment to moment, on how fast to beat your heart; you do not dictate, moment to moment, how fast to metabolize food, these are called autonomic functions. But think about controlling your breathing and you can control exactly how fast or slow you breathe . . . and then when you're not thinking about it, your breathing goes on without any conscious awareness or effort at all, just like every other autonomic function. Breathing has true shared management. All of these autonomic functions, including breathing, are controlled by the subconscious mind -- a portion of the mental body system you have very little access to. Autonomic functions also generate every emotion -- feeling-signals that are sent to the brain to produce thoughts describing the nature of each moment and prescribing a response. This is why you often sense you have no control -- emotions arising from the subconscious, not the conscious awareness are controlling you. The subconscious occupies seventy-five percent of the total mental body because there's a tremendous amount going on in the physical and the resulting emotional worlds . . . most of which you are never aware of. But remember the one physical function you share -- breathing can become a gateway, a pathway into your subconscious mind . . . the area with so much control of your life. Throughout history it has been known to every master that working with the breathing and subconscious mind is a way of mastering life -- control how you feel, and you can control how you react/respond to everything. Co-manage the breath and you co-manage the direction of the subconscious mind, the feelings, the emotions and resulting thoughts, the reactions, the expectations . . . the very road and direction of your life. Our prayer is that you sit and observe your breathing as often as you can; share the impulse 'to breathe' and watch how it releases the control of how you feel, think and act. Become the one who is co-managing your world and do this often -- at least for some minutes every day . . . it will change your life for good.

*E*very seed represents the endless future, and a daily spiritual practice is the seed of endless wisdom. Surrounding any seed are the hard shells and thorns of protecting the future. Spiritual masters and wisdom seekers have always found themselves surrounded with distractions, deflections, disruptions and misdirection . . . the shells and the thorns that protect the vast seeds of wisdom inside. This was the role of the court jester; of the fool in the tarot -- all placed in the perfect position to create distractions and protect the seed . . . only true awareness sees through these shells and thorns and beyond to capture the vast wisdom. It's written in every epic tale and mythology of history . . . the many challenges one faces on the path. Everything that is outside you is also inside; the shells and thorns inside are your thoughts that distract, the opinions that distort, the emotions that disrupt, the half-truths that deflect and the constant misdirection. Remember this when next you ask, "Why is this always happening" -- and remember this is happening to everyone around you also. You must be compassionate when you deal with the idiot you meet in another person . . . and in yourself. The key point: whenever you experience an idiot (inside or out), search for the seed -- it's always there . . . don't get sucked into the idiocy alone and think that this is all there is. When that's ever the case, you are truly an idiot. Our prayer is that you practice each day to understand the purpose of every shell and all the thorns in your life, especially when you experience and consider the world as it appears today with all of its idiocy and foolishness. Search deeply for the seeds of each moment, they're always there, being perfectly protected . . . your search beyond the distractions and disruptions will bring a great relief of joy to your foolish reactions.

The renaissance of now, the new age of enlightenment . . . this is the time to look through new lenses at a new landscape -- a landscape that's celebrating in realms that are not measured with four dimensional logic, but take into account the unaccountable magic of relationship. You've all experienced this magic in your relations to individuals -- the unreasonable joys and unaccountable surges of energy -- now you're facing a revolution taking place beyond these individual events, taking place in the collective minds and lives of everyone. Now is where your brightness and lightness response to the world becomes crowded by celebrating the value that more lives create. It's your rapidly expanding awareness that appreciates these new connections along life's path of unrelenting evolution. This new landscape brings a need of new tolerances for sharing space, for sharing time, for allowing the relational opportunities that existed only within a family, in the past, to grow beyond those four dimensions and become the high valued opportunities you reach for in the new crowd . . . arrange for in large numbers as our numbers grow. This invites sharing in ways that yesterday's world invited having -- the ability to care for each other becomes the experience of freedom, not burden. Where as in the past, the sense of freedom came from having it all (the material dream of having everything), the evolved sensation of freedom in this new landscape, will come from being connected to everyone who has something. The future of this world is in the interactions of inclusion . . . this is a revolutionary relationship to space and time; a revolution not taking place in the measurable world, but in the magical world of relational emotions, attitudes and opinions that can change in a heartbeat. Our prayer is that you allow your 'self' to change with each heartbeat in these times and these spaces of this new landscape viewed through new lens; that you welcome the crowds that are definitely arriving at your doorstep; learn to value the freedom of sharing over the freedom of having and welcome this new found freedom that brings such joy to the renaissance.

The throat, the chamber of sacred and meaningless sounds, sits between your heart and your brain with the tongue in the middle as its agent. There's a constant balance at the base of all life that's always needing to be understood; when you understand balance you are balanced . . . the throat is the mechanism of understanding. What you think and then say; what you think and then hold to yourself; what you respond to; what's in the voice of your silence -- all of this hangs in the balance of your understanding. The human has the most complex vocal anatomy of any creature on Earth; on a physical level it includes the heart, the thymus gland, vocal cords, and the fascia that extends from surrounding the heart, then up through the neck and throat into the lower jaw and tongue. This fascia adds to the vocal anatomy by connecting and coordinating all of these mechanisms around the central vocal balance to create your authentic voice. The lower jaw and tongue are a bridge mechanism between the heart center and the brain centers in order to instantly answer the questions that are constantly arising from your coordinated higher awareness. This bridge allows you to perceive your experiences, compare them to new and ancient memories and determine accuracies and inaccuracies. Above all, there needs to be fluidity amongst all of this . . . a sensation of ease and grace as these micro-moments and decisions pass by . . . otherwise you are voiceless. Our prayer is that you practice the courage to speak from your heart; open your throat to hear your voice rejoice with grace and great meaning amongst voices that may not, and make a statement that makes a difference. Finally, sing more often than you think about it.

"Misery loves company," but what is misery, a punishment, a tool? The only time you experience existence is when you are housed in a physical form -- the body. Your physical body and world are held together by tension, pressure, stress and friction . . . all are required for physical existence to exist. Stimulation is required for movement to take place; when movement takes place, opposition is experienced; opposition produces misery, yet has potential, and potential is required before anything can actually occur. Misery is therefore a naturally occurring stimulation . . . a law of nature. When this tension, pressure, stress, and friction are being experienced as opposition -- the opposition then compels you to act -- to overcome it. As you exert to overcome its bonds, you experience a new opposition (for every action there is an equal reaction). This can go on and on and is why the Buddha said, "Existence is suffering" (is misery). There is a way to work with this misery however; this suffering the Buddha referred to has a way around it. Masters throughout time refer to this way as the 'middle path' . . . the path without extremes that can stop this pendulum's manic swinging while living a productive life. First, know that there is always an opposition to every moment and every proposition -- next, embrace them both (the moment and the opposition) equally -- then move directly to the next step -- don't look back. When you achieve the next step, embrace the new opposition and take another step. When you achieve this new step, embrace the new opposition that comes with it and take a next step forward. Misery becomes a measurement of steps taken and nothing else -- every opposition becomes your propellant . . . this is the way of a master; the balance of the positive and negative to create neutrality with achievement. Our prayer is that you are inclined to take the risk of practicing this middle path; to allow neutrality to unfold your life with balance and calm, for it is this path that arrives at your dreams coming true -- not to be blocked by the constant laws of misery, suffering and opposition . . . they will always be there by natural law . . . use them.

*L*ove is an ocean in which all life lives; it is required to support the nature of living nature. All individual identities live within this ocean; this ocean has always been here; it connects everyone to everything and everyone . . . a compelling vibration of the space between us. You only allow yourself to experience this ocean when you feel completely safe. Whoever you feel safe around, in their presence you experience the love that surrounds you . . . you say, "I love you." But this is a stretch because you've only felt safe . . . love is the awareness. Whenever you don't feel safety in the presence of another, your sensory system shuts down; you become numb to the vast ocean of love surrounding you; you make claims of dislike and even hatred . . . none of which has any truth . . . love still surrounds you. It's obvious that the key here is to experience safety -- when this happens, love is experienced. To achieve this sensation of safety, the ancient wisdom keepers taught the science of meditation, yoga, chanting, prayer and lucid dreaming to build the awareness of the eternal self, the indestructible self, called "Wahe Guru" in their language. This was a secret science, hoarded by the Brahman cast, until the time of Guru Nanak, five hundred years ago. This was a time in history of great global awakening. In the West this was the Renaissance -- the Age of Enlightenment. It was an equal awakening of consciousness in the East. Today there is a great surge of spiritual mastery and this is guiding your journey toward a sense of absolute safety. And because the physics of this universe is built on polarities, "for every action there is an equal reaction," this journey to safety creates its polarity . . .

the polarity of safety is fear. Our prayer is that you establish a practice in the ancient science of Wahe Guru; work with the resulting safety to experience the love that is everywhere always; know this experience and teach others how to feel safe; understand those who live in fear and compassionately offer them some of your safety.

Spirit is currently contained as life in three dimensions made up of atoms. In quantum mechanics you understand that an atom is spread over space until an observer observes it. The act of simple perception gathers atoms in locations and creates this entire universe as your brain receives trillions of signals every moment to organize into atomic holograms that project outside yourself . . . you call this reality. Without observers, there is nothing but an expanding super-position of possibilities with zero actually taking place. Conscious beings have the simple responsibility of becoming creative, compassionate observers . . . you are intimately connected to the very existence of this holographic reality and its future. The more you look at what you believe is real, at the deepest levels, the less and less solid it becomes; the more moldable it is. We are all one consciousness and together we can make up profound differences. Our prayer is that you engage a deeply compassionate effort to observe life in the most benevolent and peaceful ways possible; build your beliefs into perfected outcomes; join in love with others; use creative nonviolence as the basis of your vision and ride this current human mega-storm into its calming . . . like taming a wild stallion with love.

With the powers of prayer, contemplation, meditation and intuition, the universe is envisioned and manifested as a combination of material realities and non-perceivable, non-material laws and principles of nature. From this multi-dimensional activity everything first takes place at the quantum level, the level of pure essence and origin . . . then manifests into four dimensions. This process of creation is accessed, without requiring approval in any way, when you give yourself your 'immortal authority'. There are three principles of nature that belong to this authority: (1)"If you're not leaning over the edge of life, you're taking up too much space;" (2)"If you're feeling out of time, you're not in the moment;" and (3)"When you experience stress and pressure you're not at your center." Leaning over the edge of life, enters the space not yet occupied; having all the time in the world, opens the space that does not yet exist; entering the space that does not yet exist, awakens your immortal authority. Tension, pressure, stress and friction are the principles holding the material reality of space and time . . . space and time provide a contextual stage for your existential predicament . . . the predicament that lives and dies. Your immortal authority is beyond this death -- death cannot touch it -- yet it creates everything. Our prayer is that you use your power of prayer, contemplation, meditation and intuition to witness the death of death; then honor your grief all the way to realizing your reality is Spirit . . . in this reality you become your immortal authority to create the universe you dream of.

*E*very moment of your life is filled with both seeds and fertilizer. You experience each of these and then store them in your brain. Neither of these are for immediate consumption in this moment, but they can be used together to create a magnificent future. There are areas of your brain that connect these sequences and make the decisions to plant the seeds and use the fertilizer. The seeds are for planting and will become consumables as they grow to fruition. The fertilizer, usually manure (the shit that happens in life), is for feeding and growing these seeds. If either of these are consumed in the moment, then the seeds are not available for creating your future, and the manure is toxic to this and every other moment . . . it leaves you with hurt feelings and a bad taste. There are parts of your brain that can be trained to either become hurt and hopeless, or understanding and inspired. Make the choice; when you find yourself in the grasp of the common sensations of feeling hurt, toxic and without a future, look at the sequences you are practicing . . . look at how you've interpreted your moments. Consciously and methodically rearrange the sequences of your experiences -- shift your interpretations -- prepare the future by planting your seeds in the manure that is dumped on you. Nourish these seeds, remain grateful, remain clear, remain ever hopeful like the zero card of the tarot . . . be the 'Fool' that observes each moment from the position of its advantage. There are parts of your brain that can make these connections and take these advantages in real time. Our prayer is that you use your brain to make the decision for taking advantage of every moment; practice knowing the difference and value of both the seeds and the manure that always collect in life; never take offense to either one of them, but use them both to build the future of your dreams . . . when people call you foolish and naive -- use their criticism as the richest fertilizer ever.

Sometimes when you turn something around, you see it in a different light, from a different angle, and this new perspective causes even a threat to lose its threatening nature. Sometimes when you're taking something the wrong way, it appears threatening even where there is no threat. Fixation on an opinion does not allow for any changes to occur in these angles or perspectives . . . the process becomes exclusive, not inclusive, and exclusive can be ruthless . . . inclusion is usually very healing. There's a place for exclusivity, just as there's a place for inclusion, yet the fundamental nature of the human being is social and therefore inclusive. Any program that teaches us to include each other is helpful to this basic human nature, value and health. Mythic themes often told of the battles between those who were able to share everything and those who wanted "it" all for themselves. The dominant archetypes and super-heroes in these tales were recognized for their inclusive collective campaigns. History shows us that every culture that made more importance of who was at the top of the power structure than the conditions of the masses, ultimately failed. Our prayer is -- in today's atmosphere of leaders battling for iconic recognition, and the fear promoted onto the migration of unknown human-ity all around us, and the fixation on differences rather than similarities -- that you change and play with the angles of your own perception, shed new light on all of these and other topics, weigh the benefits to the 'most' people rather than the advantages to the 'few' and teach this way of viewing 'space & time' to everyone you meet . . . just as the great masters throughout history did. Become the human being who is being humane -- you have this authority to make a great difference.

The word FORGIVE is one of the compound words made up of other words. The two words within it are -- FOR and GIVE. FOR is a shortening of the word FORWARD and GIVE stands on its own. The word FORGIVE means to GIVE FORWARD from a point in time, usually in the past that no longer exists . . . to this present moment, the only moment that is alive. When we FORGIVE, we reload discarded parts of ourselves that have been assigned, stuck if you will, to hold memories and grudges in empty dead space . . . forever it seems. Until we go through the process of reclaiming these parts, they are unable to be used for anything except holding these empty dead spaces with memories. FORGIVENESS is one of the most powerful tools in the process of self-empowerment and it is a selfish act . . . in the very best way, for it actually involves no one but you. It teaches you to include all of you in this moment of now, which is a nourishing and healthy process. It's like digestion, it's very personal . . . the fires of digestion fulfill the need to self-nourish. Life is a balance, a wish to honor the infinite potential through the turbulence and calm of finite matter, and dealing with the specifics that always surround the self and others. In this play, errors are guaranteed to happen, which gives rise to the need to forgive both the small dramas and the far larger traumas. Our prayer is that you realize the nature of natural growth is the production of unknowns from knowledge . . . and the corrections of the errors that must follow; that this is the price of all growth; that growth is the assignment and purpose of all life, and that forgiveness allows you to live fully . . . while growing into the gift of your life.

Spacetime is so incredibly vast; beyond imagination and made up of worlds upon worlds, galaxies upon galaxies, universes upon universes, forms upon forms of time interacting with multiple dimensions of space. It's been communicated in the teachings of the ancient wisdom keepers that one must hold the space that is not yet occupied, in order to open the space that does not yet exist. This space, the one that does not yet exist, is located in a place known only to your deeper senses (rasa in Sanskrit) that are not yet active. In this world you always receive that which is scheduled for you, but not yet present. In this way, your effortless effort responds to the waves of time . . . the moments in these waves are your moments . . . they exist where all that is desired is scheduled to be delivered. Your life within this realm works exactly the way the heart works in your body -- there is a devoted exertion to give everything and then a complete relaxation to receive it all back. This total devotion places your total self-value into play, then with total relaxation, you receive your desired due right back . . . what goes around comes around. This practice allows you to realize the grand patterns of the cosmos; the space not yet existing, the gates to this space, the keys to open them and the mastery of it all. When this becomes your life's meaning, it so outperforms the programming of the jobs, the cars, and the houses, that it maintains all these things without focusing on them. This is the true treasure, the mythic archetypal template containing levels of effortless adventure in your abundant journey through life. Our prayer is that you open up the pages to this adventure of omnipresence, walk into the spaces not yet occupied and then enter the spaces that do not yet exist . . . you will be opening the book of your life . . . to the chapters of the time of your life.

You are a gathering of breaths . . . breaths of existence collected into a body of spacetime for the purpose of fulfilling a conscious awareness driven by the promise of a universal soul. Waves upon waves of prana (life-force) carry you through a labyrinth of incarnations . . . your lives 'ever' rising from your deaths 'never' happening form the path you are traveling through this myriad of illusions. Lessons wind through the mysteries of space toward the mastery of time, and with each of these lessons you gather more of your essential code . . . the code of being you. Each grave error you commit simply adds gravity to live within . . . then it's resolved, ultimately, by the levity you acquire in perfecting the process. If practice makes you perfect, then it's perfection that keeps driving you to practice. Meeting the parts of you that need nothing except being you pushes you forward, while the parts of you that require confirmation from everything around you, hold you back. Life is the collection of results over the centuries and millennia and ultimately fills itself with itself; overflows and shares itself with everything else, and makes up for all the gross errors of space with calculations of perfect timing. Our prayer is that you allow this great mechanism to continue to honor the imperfections that cause the uniqueness that makes you -- you; to allow yourself to excel within this imbalanced balance and enjoy the path of growing -- from the terrible mistakes, and grave errors, plus the extraordinary experiences and amazing miracles -- toward the person who innocently and ecstatically gathers the breaths of existence where it all began.

There's a wave of time moving everywhere always; it's a wave to anywhere from right where you are. You can either ride this wave, or try to push this wave, or you can try to avoid and pull away from this wave. The quality of your life will depend on how you ride and relate with this wave . . . or don't. From the early archetypal wisdom of ancient societies grew the world's mythologies, mantras and yantras and their deeply profound testimonies. They were based on these waves of time and how your skills of riding them were to be developed and used. The ingenious nature of mythos, mantras, yantras, mandalas, hieroglyphs and ideograms kept this higher evolutionary memory alive throughout time with their stories. 'Memory triggers' that stimulate 'receptor codes' unlocked and decoded the mysteries held in these waves as societies evolved and individuals excelled. Yantras are the visual equivalence of mantras; science studies, some using my wife and I in MRI tubes, have proven that the combinations of mantras, mudras and yantras produce blood flow to areas of the brain that inspire understanding, balance physical gravity with emotional levity, and mimic the nature of human nature with the far more compatible and comprehending cosmic nature. Mantras, yantras and the like, allow you to ride these waves of time right at the balance point; anchored at the grounding point, while leaning and moving into the direction of your desired point of destiny. Our prayer is that you develop a daily practice of mantra, mudra and yantra; create something that you say and something that you see each day to inspire your inspiration as you ride the waves of your time throughout the oceans of your life with great levity. Catch the wave.

*S*ince life is a circle, you need to add levity otherwise gravity turns it into a downward spiral. Youth guarantees levity, but as you age, you must add conscious awareness. Add it intentionally with yoga, meditation and prayer through all circumstances. Our prayer is that you levitate intentionally, emotionally and mentally every day.

When tragedy strikes at any moment, it is helpful to remember -- "That which can be imagined can happen, and all that happens, begins with the imagination . . . positive and negative." Einstein once said, "Imagination today is reality tomorrow." It is time to use the universal law of equal and opposite to create a collective imagination that is equal and opposite to the imagination that is creating tragedies . . . to use the laws of this universe and produce a universal calm with peace. It is time to progress toward a tipping point -- use the higher powers of the higher mind and collectively envision solutions. It is vitally important to know what the challenges are -- it is equally vital to set your imagination free to roam the dimensions for discovering the solutions that have been hidden until now. Einstein also said, "I use paper for memory and my brain for discovery." Journal every possibility, no matter how farfetched, turn your brain into an imagination generator and free your mental power to discover more . . . don't hold it back. The answers are right here, right now, and are waiting for you, me, and every one of us to discover. If the problem is there, which it is, the solution must also be right there . . . it's the law of nature . . . "For every action there is an equal, opposite reaction." Once you know the tragedy, don't continue to occupy your mental space with its repetitive telling, for this will occupy the vision that can be used to imagine the solutions. Our prayer is that you know that you know . . . you know that you matter . . . you know that you know the solutions that matter; that you become the leader you were born to be and become the change you want to see. Our prayer is that you take your imagination; add it to the collection of all of us;

become a tipping point of compassion, where the universal laws of equal and opposites produces the complete opposite to these tragedies. It can be done . . . imagine it . . . it will happen . . . time is waiting for us.

*T*he constant option in every moment is the next moment, and the next, and the next . . . there is always the ability to remake what is . . . into what is to be. Our prayer is that you are skilled in using 'what is' as the raw material of what is to become.

*L*ife expresses itself through your finite body-glove as it's driven through your unique path of an infinite-oath, a kind of promise, by the Soul. You live through 8.4 million pre-human incarnations, and then 84,000 human births. Everyone starts out as mineral, through hundreds of thousands of lifetimes while you travel from the most opaque, to the translucent, and into the metals. You then pass through millions of plant lifetimes, progressing from the basic to the very complex. Throughout your next level, the animal births, you master their incredibly powerful expressions. Each of these existences has mastery, a series of events, as part of the total of human characteristics. You are being prepared with countless lessons for your human evolution toward enlightenment. Yogi Bhajan once said, "It really doesn't matter if you believe in reincarnation or not . . . it happens anyway." All these creatures, plants and minerals, even now, deliver their messages and subtle reminders to your journey of the Soul . . . Are you noticing? For example, the message of a dog is loyalty; the opaque rock is steadfastness; the diamond is sheer clarity; the dolphin tremendous joy; the horse, to be direct -- a horse always knows where it stands. Our prayer is that you accept your current life as a part of an incredibly vast chain of events; learn from every moment you experience while blessing and receiving every one of every kind (minerals, plants, animals, insects and people) that experiences each of these moments with you. Fully fill this moment right here, right now . . . you've been born so many, many times . . . trust yourself, you have all these skills . . . you know how it's done.

What you see when you look through your eyes is a combination of what you see and how you see. Your observation of another person, for example, through your eyes alone doesn't see who they are -- you slightly see who they are, but it's highly distorted by who you wish they were. The only way in which you can actually observe someone or something else, is to look through your eyes . . . then look through their eyes. And the only way you can ever look through someone else's eyes, is to surrender your eyes. Now that's a scary proposition because your eyes are constantly telling you who you think you are, so when you surrender your eyes to see through someone else's, you no longer feel like you know who you are. There's an upside to this however, for when you no longer know who you are via your senses, that's when you're able to truly KNOW who you are without any sensory reasons. It's called 'unreasonable knowing' . . . you are in fact everything. This is your inner guidance. This vast unreasonable capacity was known to the ancients as the 'infinite stranger', also your 'immortal authority'. It displays the most exalted version of your 'self' -- usually unknown to you until you die . . . that's a huge surrender. However, there's a way to surrender to this most perfect version of you while yet alive. It comes to life within a daily consistent practice of deeply knowing plus surrendering your version of the vision . . . seeing the world through the perspectives of others. Our prayer is that you produce a high value awareness as your foundation; then surrender your point of view, your version of the vision; incorporate other angles . . . the perspectives of others. Relate to life through this expanded perception and become your immortal authority . . . become your more infinite self . . . don't be a stranger, you've always been there . . . surrender to you.

The human tongue is the most complex muscle system in your body . . . there's a reason for this. This tongue contains seventeen separate muscle groups allowing your vocal anatomy to create the complex sounds of language . . . there's a reason for this. The tongue and the heart are physically connected through meridians . . . there's a reason for this. With your complex vocal anatomy, the human is the only animal able to utter a consonant . . . all other creatures are able to express with vowels. Vowels make all the sounds, consonants create the directions these sounds travel through . . . internally and externally. Vowels, consonants, sounds and directions are the roots of mantra . . . the vocal projection of your mind. The universe demonstrates extreme balance; the grand patterns at the highest levels of the cosmos -- are equal to the personal patterns at your own level -- are equal to smallest patterns at the quantum levels . . . bridges upon bridges upon bridges act as pathways of awareness, intelligence, understanding and connection. Sound naturally and equally affects all of these levels, music is a harmonious form of sound; language is a meaningful form of sound; mantra is an effective combination of sound, language and music. Our prayer is that the power of your voice, coupled with the science of your awareness, added to the song of your life, produces the mantras of your choice, to free your expression from the slavery of voicelessness . . . use your tongue . . . express yourself with your highest expression.

Subatomic particles are the tiniest elements of matter . . . smaller than an atom they include electrons, protons, neutrons, six types of quarks ('up', 'down', 'bottom', 'top', 'strange', and 'charm'), bosons, photons, neutrinos and gluons that hold them all together. Photons and neutrinos are produced in huge quantities from the sun and other stars, while the rest are components in all matter. At this subatomic level, called quantum measures, every particle of space and moment of time contains the potential for everything . . . both the trash and the treasures are always available at this threshold of existence. Particle physics and nuclear physics are the modern studies of the logic of these particles. Metaphysics is the ancient study of the magic of these particles . . . known as the 'treasures' of prakriti. Both systems are aware that the pathway to these treasures has a cost. In modern physics the cost is known as, "for every action there's an equal reaction." In metaphysics this cost is defined as the path you navigate through the world's disruptions to arrive at the sanctuary of your treasures. In both physical and metaphysical technology, at this quantum core level of physical matter, it's been found that sound has a profound affect. Sound is the foundation, a bridge between the spiritual sciences of the ancients and the common sciences of the modern times. For example, modern medicine finds great results with sonograms, while metaphysics changes life through mantra. Our prayer is that you realize the balance between the trash and treasure in your life; use the sound of your own voice to influence which you want to experience at the quantum core level of your world, and be grateful that all paths can lead to whatever you desire.

When you are aligning your consciousness into a state of awakening, your body cells enter a space of great ease. Here there is very little perceived tension, pressure, stress or friction; you are centered, balanced and equal to all tasks. Our prayer is that you dwell in this space of effortless effort and bask in the joy of the ease.

A picture of the eye of the universe, the realm of the deep central sun, is identical to the patterns in the iris of your two eyes, yet a full understanding of the magnitudes of this realm make no sense to these two sensory organs, it only makes sense to your 3rd eye. What you experience as your experience in life is as unique as this pattern in your iris, and at your fingerprints . . . yet at the level of the awareness that the third eye perceives -- nothing is different . . . everything around you is connected to you . . . virtually the same as you. This is the riddle of reality, and the reality of the riddle. What you experience with your senses all around you, are the three and four-dimensional attractions of your life. These attractions are also the three and four-dimensional distractions standing in the way of the awakening of your higher consciousness. Throughout the history of spirituality, the seekers thought that these three and four dimensions must be avoided. They were considered disruptive and stifling to the consciousness. And yet, try as they might, they could not escape. Along comes the concept of grishtha ashram (enlightened house-holding). If you create a practice to conscientiously breathe and meditate deeply each day, you will eventually find that these dimensions are not distractions at all, but the keys to decoding the riddle. There's a saying, "No matter where you go, there you are." When your meditations accept living in a physical world dominated by third-dimensional space and fourth-dimensional time, you then relax with these attractions/distractions and discover the keys and doorways to the riddle's code. Our prayer is that you master these keys and doorways with your meditations; hack the codes that hold the riddles with your mantras; enable your destiny to fully awaken; explore the eye of the universe . . . and be you being you.

Ninety-five percent of the known universe is the unknown and invisible sub-substance is called dark matter and energy. It's what is surrounding all universes, galaxies, stars, this solar system, and your body . . . keeping them together and operating. No one has ever been able to observe it; it's regarded as exotic; it's moving in extra dimensions; a quantum version of equilibrium . . . all of this is true. But tens of thousands of years ago, mystics, seers and yogis knew in their meditations, this invisible sub-substance is actually the recycled, re-materialed invisibility that emerges from the black holes (of recycling) through the white holes (of re-entry). It's the reconstituted sub-subatomic substance -- the raw materials for building atomic structures. In other words, they said in their language: black holes are the force of Shiva, the destroyer (tearing everything down to nothing -- to dark matter) and the white holes are the force of Brahma, the creator (producing all things brand new from nothing -- using dark energy). The visible world is the force of Vishnu, the sustainer, maintaining the mechanisms of matter. Think about the magnificent balance that exists at this invisible level of nature. Remember this when you experience the significant imbalance that exists around human nature. It's the conscious awareness and a visceral relationship with these deep realities of universal nature that allow you to anchor in them, balance on them, ride with them, and use them to navigate the turbulent waves of the human imbalance. Those ancients referred to this invisible dark-matter and dark-energy as angelic forces . . . it is there to serve you when you relate to it. Our prayer is that you take advantage of this invisible advantage . . . have a deep connection to that which is right there, yet not measurable . . . generate the faith and trust that it takes to connect, command and use this invisible force more fully to generate angelic balance in your life.

You are a broadcast of 'light & sound' -- driven by the Soul -- occupying and experiencing your sensory body -- all to observe what appears as a physical world. Your destiny establishes how this broadcast unfolds over the period of your life on Earth and your courage influences this destiny. Using the reality of your light-body, within the resonance of your physical body, explores the depth of your cosmic consciousness to awaken the sleeping presence of your purpose. This brings the courage to life. Legions of angels and guides, in the form of conscious fields of compassion, form around you. Your life on this Earth becomes healthier and happier in so many ways, while your efforts become more effortless. Being carefree rather than careful, you find the freedom to connect to the value of your time rather than the cost of your space. When you live in this way, you ignite the ability to possess three dimensions without being possessed by them. It's a sense of care-freedom that is your birthright on Earth. Our prayer is that you experience your care-freedom; broadcast your light and your sound; awaken your purpose; stretch into your body-glove and dance with your angelic guides as a lifestyle each day.

When the times of life make you feel like crawling under your hoody and hiding -- think on this ... Every moment of time is a point in space, and time passing is just these points switching and mixing up their positions . . . all the points are always still there, always present in the fabric of spacetime. This is both the scientific and the mystical perspective . . . and a cosmic reality as well. A mystic has a sophisticated system of viewing this reality and it was prevalent in their astronomical observations of the ancient world. Measuring great distances in the fabric of space; understanding the mechanics of great periods of time (past, present and future), and knowledge of the frequencies that regulate the structure of matter . . . all were common practice in these ancient moments in the life of a mystic. Another expression of their great genius as wisdom-keepers was their ability to encode these complex systems of knowledge with profound truths and produce a methodology to use pictures, postures, symbols, words and stories that would endure down through the ages. This formed the science of what we today call yoga, meditation, mantra and mythology. By the way, the difference between mythology and history is that mythology is true. Our prayer is that you become the mystic that you actually are; recognize this role whenever you want your hoody as a place to hide; turn such a moment into your meditation sanctuary and use it to discover ways that transform, shift and mix up the points of spacetime into alternate formations of inspiration and joy. Be the mystic. Bend the time. Shift the shape of space.

*U*ncovering the seeds of reality has always been opposed by the inherently deep protectionist nature of tradition. Mythologies recited throughout the ages have both tried to break this protection down to allow for change and maintain its closed structure to sustain the familiar. You, at every moment, have this battle going on inside and outside . . . it's what makes up the noise of the mind and the battles on the streets. Meditation is what exposes this noise and chanting is what sweeps it out the door . . . just like house cleaning. The human mouth has always been both a doorway to freedom, and the target of great restriction throughout time . . . its true power as this portal to freedom, has been attacked for eons. Throughout history, this protectionism of holding on to tradition for familiar safety, rather than opening the voice portal to the quickening of decoding life, has been blocking the seeding of human reality. Just as the flower blooms at the end of a cycle, to seed and insure the continuation of life, your life has arrived at this time within time to insure that life is alive. It is now -- and our prayer is that you recognize the profound purpose for these seeds of inspiration inside you. Open the petals of your time into full bloom; allow your mouth to speak with words that break the codes of evolution; allow humanity to prosper in peace without the differences of tradition and be the light you know you were born to be.

Imagine, if you will, the 'perfect you' -- a version of you that could exist "if only x, y & z." This version of you, plus your imagination's most far-reaching versions even beyond this, are the beginning images of your actual higher self. As a small child, you would often have these glimpses of who you could be, at your very best, at your very core, if you only had the courage to do so. You may not have had the words to fully express it way back then, but it was clear to you that it existed all the same. Remembering that every part of life is a part of every life . . . a cosmic law that explains to us that everything is everywhere always . . . this then means that you actually are -- in fact -- all those images you can imagine. This also confirms that all life can be abundant and complete, even though the common habit today is of competition and scarcity. You see . . . competition and scarcity were the habits formed when the devastating ice ages descended upon us and turned us into barbarians . . . this habit has been stuck in our human psyche as a reality, right up to today. It's up to you to break this habit for yourself; to set yourself free from all that it brings with it like: fear, scarcity, doubt, abandonment, feeling less than, being jealous of, feeling alone and every other sensation that makes you think and feel that you are not being supported by nature. Our prayer is that you practice feeling full and fully embraced when the actual sensations are making you feel empty and all alone . . . break that habit. Our prayer is also that you then take this full embrace forward and use it to fill and embrace others . . . what goes around comes around. Before too long your world will be experiencing this connection, this fullness, the abundance and the nature of nature. Begin in a small way today, for this is you reprogramming you into the higher self of you that has been right here with you all along.

In honoring the wind . . . the air . . . the breath of life; with your home of immeasurable strength within earthly matter; riding the waves of the oceans of time and possessing a golden flame in the forest of every darkness -- you are now a noble messenger of ether's wisdom. Our prayer is that you remember this is who you are and ride it to the ultimate level of your life.

Wisdom of great sages over the ages says, "Through the events of life you establish your sense of existence as a small child; your sense of authority as an adolescent, and your sense of identity as an adult." In order to establish you own identity, at the edge of space, in the middle of time, you must have a secure and courageous sense of purpose with higher guidance. This is the realm of your own 'polarity', of your 'polarity guide' if you will. When you can only experience what is right before you, your 'polarity guide' can see beyond the edges. When you're overwhelmed by memories and anticipation, your 'polarity guide' is at the very calm center of each moment. When you are not certain who you are, your 'polarity guide' identifies within the impossible to appear possible in a heartbeat. Because the polarity of the impossible is the possible, and because in this universe for every action there is always a completely opposite reaction, your 'polarity guide' is your own highest awareness and has to be right there . . . always . . . it's a law of nature. The key is to make contact and use this power . . . this takes practice. Our prayer is that you practice diligently every day: to know that your highly aware 'polarity guide' is always with you; allow the sensations of this connection to seep through each moment; gather the courage from being taken care of by such a wise, benevolent, unwavering guide . . . with you right now . . . with you right here . . . it's your right of just being born.

Confirming with the feelings of your 'emotional body', what you know with the thoughts of your 'mental body', by using the mechanics of your 'physical body', is one of the many benefits of kundalini yoga. Being able to then use the yogic mechanics of posture, breathing, chanting and moving to choose the exact thoughts and feelings is an even a more advanced usage of kundalini. The fundamental meaning of the word 'yoga' . . . to unite . . . gets your parts working together in harmony. Once united, identifying each of these aspects of your life as a separate 'body', allows you to perceive the parts individually within this unity. Like taking something apart, once it's working, to understand how it works. First you unite your life . . . get it to work accurately and efficiently; then you separate it to know how this all takes place. This is important because otherwise, having extensive awareness without extensive understanding can become a pathway to suffering. Many of the spiritual and religious traditions, throughout history, would worship suffering . . . believing it was an essential part of enlightenment. Understanding means 'standing under' . . . viewing the working relationships and allowing your awareness to escape from suffering through wisdom. Our prayer is that you are massively aware as well as being massively joyful in the same moment . . . suffering simply becomes a momentary gauge on the dashboard of your life to let you know . . . now is a time to add a little understanding into the mix.

*J*ust before the sunrise of every dawn, there's an opportunity to establish the nature of your day within the birth of the day. Known as the ambrosial hours, it's the time of communion with your prophets and guides who can see your way through every moment; it's connecting with your ancestors and angels who can see your way through life's lessons; it's joining forces with your own higher-self who can see you as you. Used by wisdom-keepers throughout time, the ambrosial hours is a time of peace and calm in which yoga, meditation, prayer, chanting and all forms of joyfulness and contemplation can set the momentum of who you are within the moment of when you are. Our prayer is that you take advantage of this advantage as often as it's possible and eventually you'll be making the impossible -- possible; the possible -- actual, and the actual -- memorable . . . just by being present with you in the wisdom of you.

The web of a spider is like the structure of an awakened human's life -- precise, gentle, dramatically strong, and patterned with highly geometric symbololology . . . the abode of unusually accurate wisdom that's able to capture the nourishment of any moment . . . "good" or "bad". The web of an awakened human is the web that has no weaver . . . it's simply spun and woven from the vast universal awareness. This web is a constant confirmation that you're unbreakable; unable to be disappointed; unable to be discouraged -- all because when you are this conscious, you're aware of your incredible 'self'. You're unable to be insulted, offended, bullied, or denied because you are just so deeply unwilling to fall for the tricks of life. This unwillingness is actually a measure of your dedication to the nature of life -- the nature that's woven into all parts . . . the offensive; the insulting; the disappointing; the discouraging are all a set up to be upset . . . the illusion of the great trickster. And when you've got no reason to be upset -- it's impossible for you to be set up. You don't attempt to explain away any such moment, you simply allow the moment to speak for itself . . . the nature of your mastery is that you listen deeply. Our prayer is with your incredible self; with your masterful approach to each moment; with the web that connects you to all that is, and the realization that every challenge is placed in your web to strengthen it . . . you're never tricked by the trickster -- you just listen deeply.

Our Prayer is for your
Many Blessings

Made in the USA
Monee, IL
13 August 2022